MW00911321

BROOME COUNTY

COUNTY

I M A G E S

Broome
County
IMAGES

By Karen Hammond
Corporate Profiles by Suzanne Meredith
Featuring the photography of Kirk and Lesli Van Zandbergen
Contributing photography by Stephen J. Appel and Ed Aswad

Produced in cooperation with
the Broome County Chamber of Commerce

Staff for *Broome County: Images*
Publishers: Ronald P. Beers and James E. Turner
Publisher's Sales Associate: Lisa Lunger
Acquisitions: Henry S. Beers
Executive Editor: James E. Turner
Senior Editor: Mary Shaw Hughes
Managing Editors: Wendi L. Lewis and Barbara F. Harrington
Profile Editor: Lenita Gilreath
Design Director: Scott Phillips
Designer: Matt Johnson
Production Artists: Matt Johnson and Lenita Gilreath
Photo Editors: Matt Johnson, Wendi L. Lewis, and Barbara F. Harrington
Production Manager: Jarrod Stiff
Editorial Assistant: Amanda J. Burbank
Contract Manager: Christi Stevens
National Sales Manager: John Hecker
Sales Coordinator: Annette Lozier
Proofreaders: Angela Mann and Amanda J. Burbank
Accounting Services: Sara Ann Turner
Printing Production: Gary G. Pulliam/DC Graphics
Pre-press and Separations: Artcraft Graphic Productions

Community Communications, Inc.
Montgomery, Alabama

James E. Turner, Chairman of the Board
Ronald P. Beers, President
Daniel S. Chambliss, Vice President

© 1999 Community Communications
All Rights Reserved
Published 1999
First Edition
Library of Congress Catalog Number: 99-27811
ISBN Number 1-58192-007-5

Every effort has been made to ensure the accuracy of the information
herein. However, the author and Community Communications are not
responsible for any errors or omissions which might have occurred.

FOREWORD

Broome County Images is our contribution to the community. We set out to publish a book that promotes a positive image of Broome County and believe it does, in fact, give genuine testimony that this is the place to live, work, and conduct business.

Residents of Broome County should be very proud. From the natural beauty and cultural delights to the abundance of recreational attractions and top educational institutions, the region provides an unsurpassed quality of life that anyone would be proud to call home. Within these beautiful pages, it is our sincere hope that you experience the quality, texture and healthy pulse of Broome County.

The Broome Chamber and its Board of Directors felt it was time to showcase our region's achievements, progress, and the businesses and people who make positive things happen. It is with a great sense of pride and enthusiasm that we present *Broome County Images*.

We guarantee that this book captures the essence of the area, the people, the progressive partnerships, and the exciting opportunities here in Broome County. And, you will understand why our future is so bright. We are proud to share with you a glimpse into the heart and soul of Broome County—a great place to live, work, and do business.

Richard J. Lutovsky
President & CEO
The Broome Chamber

David Birchenough
Chairman of the Board
The Broome Chamber

PREFACE

There are so many things to love about the Broome County area that researching and writing this book quickly became a sentimental journey. Broome County means something different to everyone, of course, and for me the very name evokes sensory images that will remain forever: Playing in a county park with my children and the feel of damp grass beneath my bare feet; the October spectacle of hills covered in crimson and magenta; the salty-spicy taste of spiedies from an outdoor grill; the sounds of music—from opera to jazz to the cheerful summertime tinkle of a carousel tune; the crisp, sharp smell of the air when the first snowstorm blankets the valley.

Although it is impossible to thank by name all who have contributed to this book, either officially as a media representative for a business or institution, or simply because they had an anecdote or an interesting bit of information to share, they have my heartfelt appreciation. None is responsible for any errors that may have inadvertently crept into the manuscript.

This book also owes much to those who call Broome County home and who, through their involvement in local academic, civic, religious, and leisure organizations, make it a warm and nurturing place in which to establish a career and raise a family. Through good times and bad, the citizens of Broome County remain its greatest asset and its most enduring image.

Karen T. Hammond
Author

TABLE OF CONTENTS

p a r t

TABLE OF CONTENTS

part

part

1

BROOME
COUNTY
IMAGES

Photo by Van Zandbergen Photography.

WHERE RIVERS
FLOW TOGETHER

Photo by Ed Aswad, Carriage House Photography.

Previous page: The beauty of Broome County is viewed at the confluence of the Susquehanna and Chenango Rivers. Photo by Ed Aswad, Carriage House Photography.

Below: Endicott War Memorial. Photo by Van Zandbergen Photography.

Once there was only sparse vegetation and a valley formed by retreating glaciers. Migrating animals—mastodons and mammoths among them—wandered into the valley, soon followed by nomadic big-game hunters, probably the first human beings to see the area we know today as Broome County.

Between 5000 and 3000 B.C. the climate moderated and nut-bearing deciduous forests gradually replaced the early conifers. Together with rivers that had formed along glacial meltwater corridors, they supported a variety of wildlife including deer, wild turkeys, and rabbits. Plants flourished in the now lush valley, providing the inhabitants with an abundant food supply.

The nomadic tribes began a transition that took them from lives as wanderers to new traditions. As hunter-gatherers they moved not just to follow migrating animals, but also to take advantage of plentiful fish in the nearby rivers, and, in season, a bounty of wild plants and nuts. Archaeologists from the Public Archaeological Facility at Binghamton University have found evidence of the tribes' existence in flint spear points and other early artifacts discovered along the Chenango River. And where the Chenango and the Susquehanna flow together at Binghamton, the site of a fishing camp has yielded net sinkers used to weigh down fishing nets.

By A.D. 800, the nomadic way of life had all but come to an end. The tribes settled in one area and began to focus on fishing and on growing the "three sisters"—squash, corn, and beans—so important to Native American life. Remains of the "three sisters," the first archaeological evidence of agriculture in the area, were uncovered in the 1960s in a primitive refuse pit excavated at Roundtop, now an Endicott family park.

With settlement came territorialism. Stockades were built to protect several sites, including one at Castle Creek in the Town of Chenango, and the tribes began to band together. They built their first permanent buildings, structures known as longhouses that sheltered several families, and established the Iroquois Confederacy. After 1714 this became known as the League of Six Nations, banding together the Delaware, Nanticoke, Oneida, Onondaga, Shawnee, and Tuscarora tribes. Their primary settlements were at Onaquaga, near what is now Windsor, and Otsiningo, near Binghamton.

Explorers, fur traders, and missionaries arrived around 1700, exposing the Native Americans for the first time to European influences. Onaquaga became a stopping-off point en route to Fort Orange, now Albany, which had been established as a trading post. In 1998, an Iroquois settlement excavated in the town of Dickinson near Broome Community College yielded evidence that by the mid-18th century the Iroquois were actively engaged in trade. The old flint hunting points had been replaced, at least in part, by brass, indicating that the indigenous people were recycling materials they had traded with white settlers.

The first written documentation of the area's Native Americans comes from journals kept as early as 1737 by Conrad Weiser, a Pennsylvania diplomat, who noted that their settlements could be

Above: A Native American demonstrates his unique skills.

Below: Handmade Indian baskets produced by the native Americans are one of the most sought after crafts in the area. Photos by Van Zandbergen Photography.

found from the confluence of the Susquehanna and Chenango rivers to present-day Chenango Forks. The Fort Stanwix Treaty Conference of 1768 established the boundaries of the Native American and white settlements, protecting Native American enclaves in Onaquaga and Otsiningo from the white settlers.

Just a few years later, the looming American Revolution drove a wedge into the League of Six Nations. Some Native Americans, under the leadership of Chief Joseph Brant, who used Onaquaga as a base, sided with the British; others opted to help the colonists, with whom they remained on good terms. Apparently fearing that those tribes friendly to the British were increasing in strength, George Washington ordered the Clinton-Sullivan expedition of 1779—led by Major General John Sullivan, with the New York contingent led by General James Clinton—to move into and take control of the region in order to cut off supplies to the British. In his book *The Valley of Opportunity* (Donning, 1988), Broome County Historian Gerald Smith describes what happened:

"As Clinton approached the confluence of the Chenango and Susquehanna rivers, his troops sought to destroy the local Indian villages. Since Onaquaga had been destroyed previously [by Colonial forces under Col. William Butler], Otsiningo remained as the sole target. When his forces arrived, however, they found the

The heavenly view from Roundtop Park allows families to enjoy the grandeur of nature.

site already burned. A few scattered Indian homes were destroyed and Clinton moved toward the west, meeting Sullivan's forces in the future Broome County at what became Union, New York."

Many of the remaining Native Americans moved north to Canada. Seeing the potential of the verdant valley, white settlers moved in quickly. A group of Massachusetts speculators made the "Boston Purchase" of more than 230,000 acres, encouraging many New Englanders to come to the area.

A parcel of 30,600 acres at the confluence of the rivers, encompassing what are now parts of Binghamton, Conklin, Kirkwood, Union, and Vestal, was granted to James Wilson and William Bingham of Pennsylvania and to Robert Hooper of New Jersey. The book *Binghamton and Broome County, New York* (Lewis Historical Publishing Co., Inc., 1924), edited by former Broome County Library Director William Foote Seward, notes that after the three men divided the land among themselves, Bingham owned the eastern end of the purchase. Although Bingham never laid eyes on the land that would eventually bear his name, his land agent, Joshua Whitney, quickly got to work. Historians give Whitney credit for carving a village out of what had been wilderness. Court and Water streets were laid out, and a courthouse, complete with jail cells and a sheriff's residence, went up on land Bingham had donated as a public square. Chenango Point, as Binghamton was then called, was soon a booming village in Tioga

County. In 1806 a new county was separated out of Tioga County and named for John Broome, one of the organizers of the Sons of Liberty in New York City, a lieutenant colonel in the Revolutionary War, and later lieutenant governor of the state.

By the early 1800s there was weekly mail service via a post rider, a variety of small shops served the population, and ten physicians had set up practice in the village and surrounding areas. A newspaper, *The American Constellation*, was published in 1800-1801. *The Broome County Patriot* was established in 1811; by the time it folded in 1820, it had a rival, *The Republican Herald*. This was replaced by *Broome Republican*, forerunner of today's *Press & Sun-Bulletin*. A subscription library opened in Binghamton in 1801, followed by a library established in Lisle in 1815.

The entire county enjoyed ready access to the rivers that provided convenient transportation for goods and lumber, and Chenango Point, the Broome County seat, was proving to be especially well situated to carry on a brisk trade. Since the late 1700s the bustling county seat had sometimes been referred to as "Binghamton" in honor of William Bingham, and in 1834 a decision was made to make the name official and to incorporate the village of Binghamton with attorney Daniel Dickinson as its first president.

Beautiful architecture is bountiful in the local municipal buildings in Broome County. All Photos by Van Zandbergen Photography.

Broome County was on the move. Dickinson and others had been instrumental in bringing the railroad to the area, and the Chenango Canal connecting Binghamton with Utica was completed in 1837. Together they helped open up the valley to new businesses. The population increased quickly, including many European immigrants who came to work in the newly developing industries and brought with them the work ethic and skill levels that define the area to this day. Public schools and several new churches, including two churches for black citizens, increased in number to serve the burgeoning population of the county's largest area. Binghamton's first synagogue was organized in 1855 and met in several temporary locations before erecting a 300-seat wooden building in 1899 on Water Street.

Growth continued, although at a slower pace, during the period of the Civil War. The citizens of Broome County threw themselves into the war effort, providing lumber and other goods and shipping them via the Erie Railroad and the Chenango Canal. After the war there was more reliance on the fast, efficient railway system, and the canal closed in 1877.

The years following the war were again a time of rapid expansion for Broome County, as they were for much of the rest of the country. In 1867, Binghamton, now with a population of 11,000 residents, became a city, with Abel Bennett as its first mayor. The industrial base grew to include furniture manufacturing, including a factory run by the famous Gustav Stickley and his brothers, wagon making, steam-engine production, several breweries, and

**H.B. Endicott Courtesy of Broome County
Historical Society.**

Endicott and Johnson historic postcard courtesy of Broome County Historical Society.

George F. Johnson Monument statue pays homage to a key player in the Broome County growth. Photo by Van Zandbergen Photography.

leather-tanning operations. A whip business begun in 1854 by Adin Coburn in Windsor continued to thrive and would last a century. Dr. Kilmer's famous "Swamp Root" patent medicine was produced in Binghamton beginning in 1879, an operation that would continue until the early 1940s. Cigar production, which by the turn of the century employed five thousand local residents, brought the area international recognition as the second-largest cigar manufacturer in the country.

Although industries had been concentrated in Binghamton, they began to move into other parts of the county. A retail shoe company begun by Horace Lester in 1850 in Binghamton moved in 1888 to Lestershire, which became the Village of Lestershire in 1892 and Johnson City in 1916. In 1900, Lestershire Manufacturing Co. was renamed Endicott-Johnson Corporation after its founders, Henry B. Endicott and George F. Johnson, respectively the former principal stockholder and the manager at Lestershire Manufacturing. Endicott-Johnson's first tannery opened in 1902; over time the company expanded westward, helping to establish the neighboring village of Endicott. The company would become known around the world, employing thousands of Broome County residents, including many workers who arrived from eastern and southern Europe attracted by stories of the beauty and peacefulness of the valley and the ready availability of jobs. In a perhaps apocryphal but often repeated story, workers fresh to North American shores, eager to get to work but

An early community swimming pool. Historic postcard courtesy of Broome County Historical Society.

struggling with a new language, were said to have arrived in Broome County asking, "Which way EJ?" The influx of workers and their families contributed to Broome's greatest population increase to date. Between 1910 and 1930 the population almost doubled from 78,809 to 147,022. Later decades reflected consistent growth until 1960 when the population leveled off. The 1990 census recorded 212,160 Broome County residents.

Endicott-Johnson provided extraordinary benefits to its workers, including low-cost housing. Built between 1913 and the 1950s and purchased with low-interest loans financed by the company, many compact, solidly built EJ homes still remain in Endicott and Johnson City. The company also provided free medical care, and EJ cafeterias offered inexpensive, nutritious meals. As the business grew, George F. Johnson and other members of the Johnson family were instrumental in establishing libraries, hospitals, parks, and recreation areas throughout the area. Babies born to workers received a $10 gold piece and their first pair of shoes, while their mothers were rewarded with a $10 gold piece of their own and free baby pictures. In exchange for being treated as "working partners," company employees were expected to be completely loyal and highly productive, and virtually without exception, they were. According to some records, in 1927 EJ workers produced a phenomenal 130,000 pairs of shoes each working day.

The shoe company's influence on the area was widespread, and EJ's philosophy of offering its workers "a square deal"—higher

The area remains a true Valley of Opportunity today as Broome County prepares for a new millennium.

than average wages plus benefits that were all but unheard of at the time—greatly influenced the business philosophy of Thomas J. Watson, Sr., founder of another company that would bring world-wide attention to the area. The EJ tanneries closed in the 1960s after more than six decades of operation. In 1995, Endicott-Johnson split into two discrete entities, a retail operation known as the Endicott-Johnson Corporation, and EJ Footwear Corporation, which assumed the wholesale, manufacturing, and import part of the business.

The industry that Thomas J. Watson, Sr., would lead to inter-national renown began in 1889 as the Bundy Manufacturing Company, makers of time clocks. The company grew, merged with other companies, diversified its products, and underwent several name changes. In 1924, it was renamed International Business Machines—IBM. Its first laboratory was established in Endicott in 1934, and until its recent closing the Glendale Laboratory in the Town of Union was one of the company's premier research and development facilities. Although many IBM installations have now moved out of Broome County, it remains the area's largest employer. A major manufacturing site—IBM Plant #1—is located in downtown Endicott, and the company's impact on the economic, social, and educational climate of Broome County is still being felt.

With the establishment of Endicott-Johnson and IBM, Broome County and the Southern Tier—as the section of New York State adjacent to the Pennsylvania border became known—was often referred to as the "Valley of Opportunity." The population grew and diversified, hospitals and institutions of higher learning were built, and a variety of high-technology companies were established in the area. In 1929, Edwin Link founded Link Manufacturing to produce trainers for airline pilots, putting Broome County on the map as the home of flight simulators. Businesses were attracted then, as they are now, by the intelligent, hard-working labor force that had helped bring Endicott-Johnson and IBM to international promi-nence. The area remains a true Valley of Opportunity today as Broome County prepares for a new millennium. ■

Industrialist Thomas J. Watson, Sr. led the new millennium when he merged several of his smaller holdings in the present IBM company. Businesses continue to be drawn to this enterprising area as it enters 2000 A.D. Photos by Van Zandbergen Photography.

The splendor of Broome County is found throughout
the countryside including the pastoral Conklin Forks.
Photos by Van Zandbergen Photography.

The history of fine craftsmanship in Broome County is evident in the interior of the Phelps Mansion. Photos by Van Zandbergen Photography.

Most tourist are drawn to Broome County's many antique galleries. Photos by Van Zandbergen Photography.

Colorful antique signs adorn the local countryside in Broom County. Photos by Van Zandbergen Photography.

chapter

CAROUSEL COUNTRY!

Photo by Van Zandbergen Photography.

Photos by Van Zandbergen Photography.

All figures on Broome's carousels are "jumpers"…George W. Johnson is said to have specified that all the animals be jumpers because he wanted even the smallest and weakest of children to have an equal chance at a thrilling ride.

Whether you know them as flying horses, merry-go-rounds, or carousels, chances are you remember the childhood thrill of riding a wooden horse, mane carved into tendrils, nostrils flaring, and painted hoofs poised to carry you off on a wonderful adventure. Although they could once be found in fairgrounds and amusement parks across the country, in recent decades many antique carousels have been broken up and the individual animals sold to collectors.

Of the approximately 170 antique carved wooden carousels still in existence in North America, and the estimated 250 remaining worldwide, six may be found in Broome County. Carousel aficionados from around the world visit Broome to ride all six merry-go-rounds and to receive a special button for completing the "Carousel Circuit."

At a time when Endicott-Johnson Shoe Company was the area's largest employer, founder George F. Johnson and other family members donated the carousels to the parks of Broome County with two stipulations: the local municipality must be responsible for their care and upkeep, and no one should ever have to pay for a ride. The carousels were among the many amenities Johnson provided the people of Broome County in the belief that as a major employer in the area he had a responsibility for his workers' total well-being. It has been said that Johnson's own childhood had little of the fun and magic he felt every child should enjoy. Through his generosity, and that of his family, children and adults still take free carousel rides at six Broome County parks from Memorial Day through Labor Day. Because of their antiquity and the fact that five of the six carousels remain on their original sites, all are listed on the National Register of Historic Places.

Broome's carousels were built between 1919 and 1934 by the Allan Herschell Company of North Tonawanda, New York, for many years the world's largest carousel manufacturer. They represent six of Herschell's remaining carousels, believed to be about 18 worldwide. Constructed at the height of the so-called "Golden Age" of carousel production, which began around 1880, all the local merry-go-rounds are built in the "Country Fair" style. Originally designed to be used at traveling shows, this type of carousel was constructed along slim, simple lines and was easy to take apart so that it could be moved from place to place. Country Fair horses traditionally have a natural, almost wild appearance, and legs that curl under them as if they are about to leap off the platform with their riders. Glass "jewels" glint in the sun and enhance their appearance. Compared to the larger, "Coney Island" style, often heavily decorated with jewels and bright paint, or the realistically proportioned "Philadelphia" style, Country Fair horses and other figures are often considered the most charming by carousel devotees.

All figures on Broome's carousels are "jumpers"—that is, they move up and down while the carousel spins. Local legend has it that this, too, came about at the insistence of George F. Johnson. Although it is more common for some of the figures to be stationary, Johnson is said to have specified that all the animals be jumpers because he wanted even the smallest and weakest of children to have an equal chance at a thrilling ride.

Binghamton's Ross Park is the site of the first of Broome's carousels, installed in 1920 and restored in 1989. Among its features are 60 horses, 2 chariots—one depicting a gorilla and one showing a maiden—and an original Wurlitzer Military Band Organ. As with the carousels at C. Fred Johnson Park and Recreation Park, this merry-go-round's figures are four abreast; they are the only remaining Herschell four-abreast carousels in the world. Visitors to Ross Park enjoy a carousel exhibit that traces the history of carousels and provides information on the six examples found in Broome County. Those who have ridden all the Broome County carousels may have a "jewel" affixed to their commemorative Carousel Circuit button at Ross Park's carousel exhibit.

The largest Allan Herschell carousel still in existence can be found at C. Fred Johnson Park in Johnson City. Installed in 1923, this most elaborate of Broome County's carousels features 72 figures backed by ornate scenic panels in a fanciful, pagoda-like enclosure. The site was formerly a large Endicott-Johnson factory complex, with the carousel erected in the employees' recreation area. Both the carousel and the two-story-high pavilion enclosing it were restored in 1993.

The only one of Broome's carousels to have been relocated can now be found at Highland Park in Endwell. Originally installed in 1925 at En-Joie Park in Endicott, another family recreation area established by George F. Johnson, it was moved to its present location in 1967. Its 36 figures include not only horses, but an unusual wild boar and a dog. The carousel also features lovely hand-stenciled support beams.

Recreation Park in Binghamton boasts still another large carousel, donated by George F. Johnson's daughter, Lillian Sweet. Its 60 figures, four abreast, jump to the music of an original Wurlitzer Military Band Organ with bells. The carousel and carousel pavilion, noted for its attractive cupola, underwent major restoration in 1990. A rededication ceremony in 1991 was attended by several members of the George F. Johnson family, including great-great-grandchildren. A statue of George F. Johnson watches benignly over the summer fun that has been his legacy since the spinning carousel was installed in 1926.

In West Endicott Park, one can ride a 1929 carousel of 36 figures. It too boasts a dog and wild boar, which are often photographed. Perhaps the most graceful of the Broome carousels, it has two baroque-style chariots. In the heyday of Endicott-Johnson, several factories were nearby and employees often met their families after work for a relaxing evening in the park.

Also in Endicott are the 36 horses and two chariots of a carousel housed in a 16-sided open pavilion and installed in 1934 for the residents of Endicott's "North Side." In an article written for the winter 1996 issue of *Yorker Magazine*, Gail Domin, executive director of the Susquehanna Heritage Area, recounts the emotional dedication of the carousel with its "charming country atmosphere," when "over a thousand neighborhood children lined up and presented Mr. Johnson with a bouquet of flowers in thanks for their new merry-go-round." The carousel is located at George W. Johnson Park.

The flying horses of Broome County have been widely photographed and written about and remain among the most enduring symbols of our area. Today, grandparents who recall attending the original dedication ceremonies and enjoying rides on the new merry-go-rounds bring their young grandchildren to the carousel parks. In a changing world the carousels continue to link the area's past to its present as each new generation of children experiences the thrill of this most magical of rides. ■

**Jewels and flowers adorn the handcrafted carousels.
All Photos by Van Zandbergen Photography.**

Hand-painted murals are a common attraction for all ages that visit the various carousels in Broome County. The carved details give likeness to a child's favorite animal. Photos by Van Zandbergen Photography.

In a changing world the carousels continue to link the area's past to its present as each new generation of children experiences the thrill of this most magical of rides.

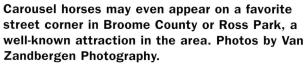

Carousel horses may even appear on a favorite street corner in Broome County or Ross Park, a well-known attraction in the area. Photos by Van Zandbergen Photography.

c h a p t e r

THE ACTIVE LIFE:
SPORTS AND RECREATION

Photo by Van Zandbergen Photography.

Summer begins its gentle slide into fall. Cool evenings follow warm days, and the hillsides are burnished copper and red. In a kind of reverse migration, cars with license plates from Florida, South Carolina, and other points south stream into Broome County, loaded with golf clubs and driven by men in colorful sports clothes. It's BC Open time!

Now a regular stop on the PGA tour, by 1999 the BC Open had a purse of $1.6 million and one of golf's most unusual trophies, modeled after a wise-cracking, club-toting comic strip character that shares the tournament's name. The comic strip "BC," about the antics of some prehistoric cave dwellers, is a creation of cartoonist and area resident Johnny Hart, a long-time supporter of Broome County's premier sporting event.

The amazing success story that is the BC Open is due largely to countywide effort. The tournament began in 1971 as a satellite stop with a total purse of $10,000. Through the vision of local businessman Alex Alexander and a host of volunteers, the tournament grew until by 1998 it had earned more than $4.8 million for local charities. Alexander stepped down as tournament director that year, to be replaced by Mike Norman. Throughout the years, enthusiastic volunteers from all over the county have been the event's life blood—some fifteen hundred donate their services each year to make the BC Open a success. Among many other duties, they host visiting players in their homes, serve as marshals, work in ticket and refreshment booths, and even baby-sit golfers' children so that spouses can attend the tournament. Although it is one of the smallest tournaments on the tour, many PGA players, themselves small-town residents, consider it one of the most friendly.

Weather permitting, BC Open week kicks off on a Monday with a pro-am tournament that gives local golf enthusiasts a chance to play with the pros. Its shotgun start, with players teeing off at all 18 holes simultaneously, sets the stage for a full week of exciting tournament play. Tuesday brings The IBM Tour Challenge , and the unique "The King is a Fink" Shortshot Contest featuring Johnny Hart and other famous cartoonists. Named for a sassy expression in the "Wizard of Id" comic strip, of which Hart is a co-creator, "The King is a Fink" contest pairs cartoonists with golf professionals. Among the many famous cartoonists who have joined Hart in pursuit of the contest purse is "Garfield" creator Jim Davis. Generous with their time, the cartoonists sign posters and other golf mementos for fans.

Previous page: Children enjoy ice skating among the many activities offered in Broome County.

Above: Favorite BC cartoon characters appear during the BC Open Golf Tourney.

Below: Tiger Woods is among the many celebrities who participate in the BC Open. Photos by Van Zandbergen Photography.

Wednesday brings another pro-am, and Thursday marks the official first round of the tournament. Following the second round on Friday, the 18th green is the site of a concert that attracts some ten thousand spectators and has featured such entertainers as Air Supply, Ray Charles, The Kingston Trio, Tanya Tucker, and Three Dog Night.

Saturday and Sunday round out the week with two days of intense professional play. The trophy has been won by such well known players as Fred Couples, Tom Kite, Hal Sutton, John Daly, Peter Jacobsen, and local favorites Joey Sindelar, Mike Hulbert, and Wayne Levi. The 1999 tournament was nationally and internationally broadcast over ESPN.

As a special bow of appreciation to tournament caddies, the BC Open hosts an annual caddy classic on the Monday following the tournament. The oldest golf tournament in the country for PGA touring caddies, it features a purse of $10,000. PGA professional golfers contribute to the purse, and some touring pros have been known to caddy for their caddies.

In the year 2000, the BC Open will move from its traditional September date to July, and will have to compete for players with the prestigious British Open. Despite this stiff competition, local golf fans, volunteers, and the BC Open staff will no doubt meet the challenge of keeping the BC Open a local sports highlight.

Summer begins its gentle slide into fall. Cool evenings follow warm days, and the hillsides are burnished copper and red. In a kind of reverse migration, cars with license plates from Florida, South Carolina, and other points south stream into Broome County, loaded with golf clubs and driven by men in colorful sports clothes.

A wide range of sporting activities is available to residents of Broome County. Photos by Van Zandbergen Photography.

Binghamton Jets, and the B-Mets baseball games bring the fans out to see the action in Broome County.

Tennis and cycling are also among the many competitive sports enjoyed in Broome County. Photos by Van Zandbergen Photography.

In winter, area sports fans cheer the BC Icemen, a United Hockey League developmental team. Broome County has a long history of enthusiastic support for hockey, beginning with the Broome Dusters who played from 1973 to 1980, the Binghamton Whalers from 1980 to 1990, and the Binghamton Rangers, an American Hockey League team that played from 1990 to 1996. A hockey booster club that began with the Broome Dusters remains active today. BC Icemen games are played at the 7,000-seat Broome County Veterans Memorial Arena in Binghamton, and offer exciting family entertainment at affordable prices.

Broome County residents are avid baseball fans, thanks in part to another legacy from George F. Johnson. As early as 1899 he was part-owner of a local professional franchise, and he later built Johnson Field, home to Binghamton baseball until 1968. Many area residents have fond memories of watching the Binghamton Triplets and such baseball luminaries as Whitey Ford, Deron Johnson, Steve Kraly, and Thurmon Munson early in their careers. The late Ron Luciano, who achieved national prominence as a colorful Major League umpire and author of several books about baseball, was a native of Endicott, as was Johnny Logan, who played for the Boston Red Sox.

Today baseball season finds fans cheering the Binghamton Mets, a Minor League baseball team affiliated with the New York Mets. Binghamton's Municipal Stadium, the B-Mets' home field, was built in 1992 and holds more than six thousand spectators.

Other sports draw avid spectators as well. The BC Jets amateur football team, one of ten teams in the Empire Football League, plays from midsummer through October at Binghamton's North Field. An annual Frito Lay/USTA Challenger tennis tournament is held each August in Binghamton's Recreation Park. Many residents regularly attend basketball, hockey, and other athletic events at Broome Community College, where an Olympic-size hockey rink is under construction, and at Binghamton University, currently a Divison II school considering application for Division I status. The university will be the site of New York State's Empire Games in the year 2000.

Throughout the county, opportunities abound for individual and team-participation sports, from cross-country skiing in winter to motocross, cycling, and running from spring through fall.

A street filled with runners is a typical site as participants push forward. Photo by Van Zandbergen Photography.

A wide range of parks provides families an opportunity to enjoy the natural surroundings in Broome County. Photos by Van Zandbergen Photography.

Serious cyclists participate in the annual Chris Thater Memorial Criterium held in late summer. Named for a Binghamton University student who was killed by a drunken driver in 1983, the race has grown into one of the most popular cycling events in the Northeast. It includes competitions for cyclists licensed by the United States Cycling Federation as well as for recreational cyclists, a road race, and an in-line skating event. Other road races, like the Lee Barta Memorial 5K, honoring slain Binghamton patrolman Lee Barta, are among several annual 5K walk-run events that offer competitive challenges while raising money for local scholarships and charities.

Many area businesses sponsor adult softball and other sports teams, while schools, various municipalities, and private associations offer a wide range of recreational and competitive sports opportunities for children and teens. The Binghamton Area Girls' Softball Association, Inc. (BAGSAI), hosts youth tournaments throughout the summer, and the Broome County Department of Parks and Recreation sponsors a senior men's softball tournament at the BAGSAI complex. Located on Front Street in Binghamton, the four-field complex, a cooperative effort between BAGSAI and Broome County Parks and Recreation, is considered one of the best in New York State.

Area parks offer year-round opportunities for family recreation. At the Town of Nanticoke's Greenwood Park, the area's largest, families find ample facilities for camping on the shores of a trout-filled lake. Picnic areas, hiking trails, and a sandy beach make the park a popular summer spot. In winter cross-country skiers swoosh along the trails while ice fishers try their luck in the frozen lake.

Popular with campers and boaters, the small Upper Lisle campground offers a New York State boat access point, as well as fishing in the Otselic River and in the Whitney Point reservoir.

Other Broome County boating enthusiasts flock to Dorchester Park in Whitney Point, which offers a boat launch and easy access to a 1200-acre reservoir. Rental boats are available, as are opportunities for swimming, picnicking, and fishing.

In summer serious swimmers head for Nathaniel Cole Park in Colesville and its 53-acre lake and huge, sandy beach. The largest facility in the county park system, Nathaniel Cole Park also offers hiking trails, picnic facilities, and rental boats.

Roundtop Picnic Area in Endicott, where so much important evidence of Native American occupation was unearthed in the 1960s, offers extraordinary views of the Susquehanna River Valley that remain much as they must have been when the area's early inhabitants roamed the land. And in Endwell, area residents enjoy swimming and other activities in the lush surroundings of Highland Park. On the Fourth of July, families flock here for a day of fun, and many bring a picnic to eat beneath the trees while they wait for dusk and a spectacular fireworks display.

Still other sites have been established to help preserve the area's flora and fauna. At Hawkins Pond Nature Area on the Pennsylvania border, for example, wildlife and plants are protected in a setting that offers picnic tables, hiking trails, and motor-free boating access. Finch Hollow Nature Center in Johnson City offers a variety of educational programs and houses an outstanding display of stuffed birds and other animals. Gardeners have long enjoyed the Cutler Botanic Gardens located at the Cornell Cooperative Extension of Broome County in Binghamton, with its rock garden, perennial displays, and ongoing teaching exhibits.

Other parks, urban and rural, and including a number of "pocket parks" offering simply a quiet bench for reading and reflection, are located throughout Broome County, all offering opportunities for relaxation or family fun. ■

Many nature admirers have found the beauty of Broome County to be the perfect locale for a retreat. Photos by Van Zandbergen Photography.

Opposite page: The Crappie Derby draws devoted out-
doorsmen to camp on the ice.

This page: Beautiful sailboats with their color and
craftsmanship are part of every lake in Broome County.
All Photos by Van Zandbergen Photography.

Chenango State Park provides many activities to area residents. Photo by Ed Aswad, Carriage House Photography.

Many people enjoy the softball complexes located in the area. Tournaments are played with a backdrop of blue-sky grandeur. Photo by Van Zandbergen Photography.

Other parks, urban and rural, including a number of "pocket parks" offering simply a quiet bench for reading and reflection, are located throughout Broome County, all offering opportunities for relaxation or family fun.

HEALTH AND EDUCATION

Photo by Van Zandbergen Photography.

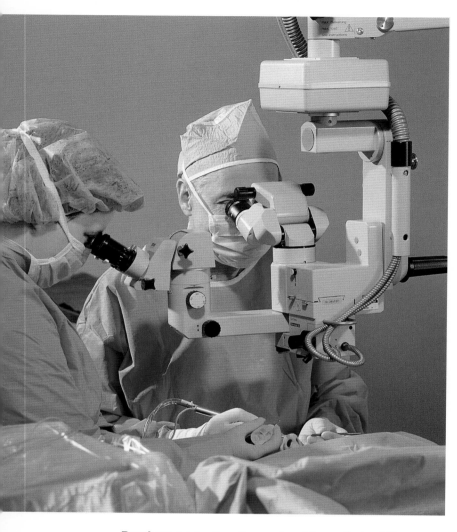

Previous page: A yellow school bus climbs hills to pick up school children in Broome County.

Above: Health care is a high priority for local residents as noted by the laser surgery in the above photo. Photo by Van Zandbergen Photography.

A safe and friendly living environment and access to good health care and quality education are usually among the first things families look for when considering a place to live. Metropolitan Binghamton, including all of Broome and Tioga counties, ranks in the nation's safest 7 percent of areas of comparable size.

Broome County residents are fortunate to have superb, comprehensive health-care facilities at Lourdes Hospital, Binghamton General Hospital, and Wilson Memorial Regional Medical Center. These are complemented by convenient offices located throughout the region to offer primary care or walk-in treatment of minor emergencies. The area's education resources offer a variety of options from private preschools to two-year undergraduate education at Broome Community College, and undergraduate and graduate opportunities through the doctoral degree at Binghamton University, one of only four campuses in the State University of New York (SUNY) system to offer the Ph.D.

Hospitals are conveniently located in the metropolitan area. Lourdes Hospital in Binghamton was established in 1925 in a former mansion on Riverside Drive. Local citizens raised funds to purchase the building and equip the hospital, which was managed by the Catholic Daughters of Charity. Today the hospital is part of the Daughters of Charity National Health System, one of the largest nonprofit health-care providers in the country.

The Regional Cancer Center at Lourdes is affiliated with the prestigious Johns Hopkins Oncology Center and offers area residents state-of-the-art diagnosis and treatment by a team of board-certified oncology physicians, specially trained nurses, and other health-care professionals.

Lourdes Primary Care Network includes more than 20 physicians' offices and walk-in services throughout the Southern Tier, and its Mission in Motion vans help bring health care into outlying areas. Among many other services, Lourdes offers an Ambulatory Surgery Center and several other specialized centers and programs focusing on concerns ranging from wellness to behavioral health, wound care, and arthritis management. Its Diabetes Center offers the area's only American Diabetes Association-certified diabetes program.

United Health Services (UHS), a community-owned, not-for-profit health-care system, provides a variety of facilities throughout Broome and surrounding counties, including Wilson Memorial Regional Medical Center in Johnson City and Binghamton General Hospital in downtown Binghamton. The area's largest provider of health-care services and its only teaching facility, UHS offers physician residencies in family practice, internal medicine, osteopathy, and podiatry. It is a leading referral center for heart, brain, and spinal surgery, renal dialysis, neonatal care, high-risk obstetrics, reconstructive surgery, mental health, chemical dependency treatment, and physical rehabilitation. The Emergency Department at Wilson is a New York State-designated trauma center.

UHS health-care providers bring services to the people of Broome through several innovative means, including a Stay Healthy program at the Oakdale Mall, where shoppers may have their weight and blood pressure checked and participate in a variety of other health screenings. UHS offers a full range of family services at several Family Care Centers, the newest located in Binghamton's downtown YWCA within an easy walk for many city residents. Its network of primary care offices and clinics receives more than five hundred thousand patient visits each year. UHS's Ideal Living Center campus includes an apartment complex for seniors and a skilled nursing facility, while United Home Care provides a variety of professional and other skilled services for homebound patients throughout the county.

In 1997, *Hospitals* magazine named UHS one of the top 100 integrated health-care systems in North America.

If good health is fundamental, so too is the opportunity for people to become all they can be through education. Broome County's public and private schools and institutions of higher learning make lifelong education an accessible reality, while other facilities throughout the county offer opportunities for learning outside the classroom.

Broome offers outstanding public school education for students from kindergarten through high school. Families also have the option of choosing among schools sponsored by various religious groups, and one nonsectarian private school.

Some Broome County schools are slowly growing more diverse, with urban schools showing the greatest percentage of minority students. In the 1998-99 school year, nearly 26 percent of students in the Binghamton school district were Black, Hispanic, or Asian. Recognizing the need to provide positive role models from a variety of ethnic and cultural backgrounds, a number of schools are initiating programs to recruit more minority faculty and staff.

County public school enrollments range from a high of about 6,266 in the Binghamton City School District to about 811 in the Deposit Central School District. Urban and rural schools alike offer special programs and resources. Binghamton High School, for example, is the site of the Rod Serling School of Fine Arts, named in honor of the *Twilight Zone* creator, who was a graduate. Here students receive instruction in the fine and per-forming arts, as well as opportunities to hone their skills in live performances. A new elementary school in Deposit has,

If good health is fundamental, so too is the opportunity for people to become all they can be through education.

Pediatrician cares for young patient and teaches him that the stethoscope has many uses. Photo by Van Zandbergen Photography.

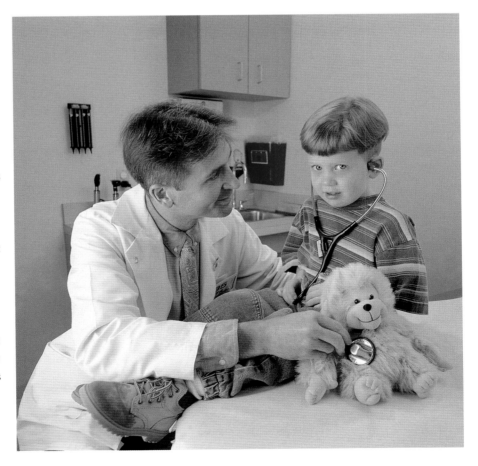

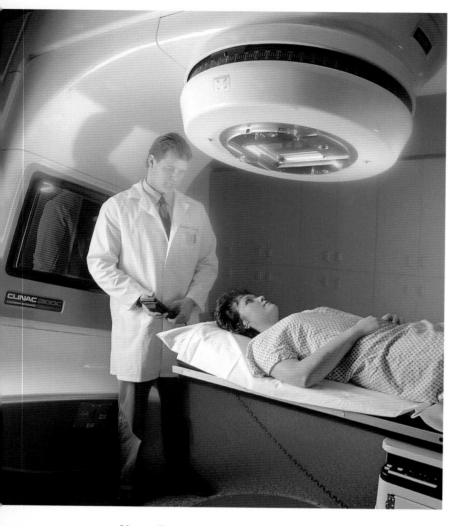

Above: Broome County residents enjoy state-of-the-art medical technology like this Linear Accelerator. Photo courtesy of Lourdes Hospital.

Opposite page: Geriatric medicine is a growing medical field for health care providers. Photos courtesy of United Health Care Services Hospital.

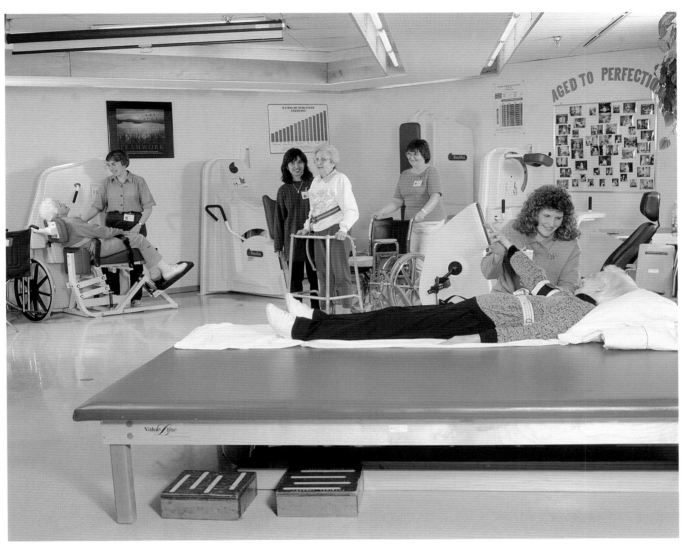

among other amenities, a state-of-the-art media center and computer lab. Large or small, urban or rural, all Broome County schools pride themselves on high academic standards.

Recent changes implemented by the New York State Board of Regents are expected to raise academic expectations even higher. Today all eleventh-graders in New York must pass the Regents exam in English in order to graduate, and fourth- and eighth-graders take comprehensive exams that test their skills in a variety of subjects. Phased in over the next few years, students will have to pass Regents exams in math, English, U.S. history, global studies, and science to graduate, plus complete more courses in math and science and earn additional credits overall.

Serving 15 school districts in Broome and Tioga counties, the Broome-Tioga Board of Cooperative Education Services (BOCES), headquartered in the Town of Dickinson, is one of 30 BOCES established throughout New York State to help public schools share services and to offer direct instructional programs. Its vocational courses range from mechanics to cosmetology, and, among many other programs, BOCES offers classes in English as a Second Language, basic education leading to the GED, a practical-nurse training program, and a variety of continuing education courses. It

provides educational and technological support and special services for area students with disabilities. BOCES also frequently collaborates with local agencies and industries to provide needed programs.

Residents wishing to go on to higher education need not travel outside the county. Both Broome Community College, whose campus is located three miles north of Binghamton, and Binghamton University, located in nearby Vestal, provide a variety of educational opportunities, while Practical Bible College in Johnson City and Ridley-Lowell Business and Technical Institute in Binghamton offer specialized training.

Broome Community College (BCC) offers 40 programs leading to associate's degrees and annually enrolls more than five thousand full- and part-time learners of all ages, including more than 100 international students from at least a dozen countries. Chartered as the New York State Institute of Arts and Sciences at Binghamton in 1946, the school became Broome Technical Community College in 1956 and Broome Community College in 1971. Traditionally strong in technology fields, today BCC offers a broad range of programs in health sciences, business, and public service. The liberal arts transfer program is BCC's largest. Its graduates are able to transfer into private and public four-year

Beautiful architecture graces the landscape of Broome County. Photo by Van Zandbergen Photography.

colleges and universities around the country, and many local residents take this opportunity to complete two years of undergraduate work at reasonable cost while living at home. Many local workers enroll in one of BCC's certificate programs to update their skills or to help make the transition into new jobs. Area residents often come to campus to cheer on one of BCC's 13 sports teams.

The college works closely with area businesses, and its specialized management or employee-training courses enroll more than two thousand employees each year. Noncredit community education courses in a variety of job-related or personal improvement subjects serve another eight thousand participants annually.

Health programs at BCC also reach into the community. One of the most innovative of these is the Decker Health Center's public dental clinic, where area residents may make appointments for free dental cleaning and evaluation. Many graduates of BCC's nursing programs staff local hospitals and other health-care facilities.

One of 64 campuses in the State University of New York system, Binghamton University provides an education so outstanding that in 1998 *Money Magazine* ranked it the fourth best college value in the nation, and *US News & World Report* called it the country's 20th-best public university. Begun as Triple Cities College in 1946 in a single building in Endicott as a way of meeting the educational needs of soldiers returning from World War II, the school later became Harpur College, and later still the State University of New York at Binghamton. Popularly known today as Binghamton University or BU, it is often referred to as "the jewel in the crown of the SUNY system."

Binghamton is a research university offering more than 130 programs of study. Each year, approximately 12 thousand students, including 19 hundred from 89 other countries, study at the university's five colleges—Harpur College of Arts and Science, the Decker School of Nursing, the Thomas J. Watson School of Engineering and Applied Science, the School of Management, and the School of Education and Human Development. Faculty members, many of whom are nationally and internationally known, write and publish frequently in their fields and many have been honored for making substantial contributions to their disciplines. Thirty-one members of the faculty have been named by the SUNY Board of Trustees as Distinguished Professors or Distinguished Teaching Professors.

Students are offered many opportunities in Broome County. Photo courtesy of Binghamton University.

The most popular majors for first-year students entering BU in fall 1998 were biological sciences, business, psychology, engineering, computer science, political science, English, nursing, and mathematics, reflective of the university's diverse academic strengths. At this "very selective" university, the average freshman enters with a grade-point average of more than 92 percent, and about 90 percent have already completed one or more Advanced Placement or college-level course in high school. Their average SAT scores are some 250 points above the national average.

BU has long prided itself on its diverse student body. Statistics released in *Inside*, a campus newspaper, indicated that students enrolling in fall 1998 came from a variety of socioeconomic, ethnic, and religious backgrounds, with 19 percent listing a language other than English as their native tongue. Binghamton graduates excel in a variety of professions, from Arnold Levine, a world-renowned cancer researcher recently named president of Rockefeller University, to author Art Spiegelman, sociolinguist and author Deborah Tannen, actor Paul Reiser, and thousands of other graduates around the

Hands on opportunities are provided for any one the many visitors to Broome County. Photo by Van Zandbergen Photography.

Everyone enjoys the opportunity to view wildlife and animals at the Zoo. Photo by Van Zandbergen Photography.

world who make substantive contributions to their chosen fields of business, technology, arts, education, and the sciences.

Many graduates choose to stay in the Broome County area. Harpur College graduates are employed in a variety of occupations within the community, while many School of Education and Human Development graduates are teachers or administrators in local schools. Others, many of whom hold undergraduate or graduate degrees in social science from the school's Human Development Division, which offers working adults convenient opportunities for part-time and evening study, are administrators in local businesses or human-service agencies. Watson School of Engineering graduates are valued employees in Broome's technology industries, and many local nurses, nurse-practitioners, midwives, and nurse-administrators hold degrees from the Decker School of Nursing. A number of area business professionals and small-business owners graduated from BU's School of Management.

The university has always had close ties with the surrounding community and is a major economic and social force in Broome County. One of the area's largest employers, it contributes more

than $300 million yearly to the local economy, offers outstanding cultural and sporting opportunities to area residents, and works closely with Broome County businesses and technological firms; its students, faculty, and staff participate in a wide variety of local service projects and charity events, and outreach programs from all of BU's schools enhance the lives of Broome County citizens in many ways.

Not all learning takes place in a classroom, of course, and Broome County offers ample opportunities to combine education with family fun. Binghamton's Ross Park, for example, is home to the Ross Park Zoo, fifth-oldest zoo in the country. Established in 1875 on land donated by local businessman Erastus Ross, its 90 wooded acres shelter a variety of mammals, reptiles, and birds.

The park's history is an interesting one, reflecting in many ways the economic ups and downs of the area. At the turn of the century, Ross Park was the place to be for Broome County families, who flocked there for amusement-park rides, picnics, and political gatherings. One of Binghamton's first electric trolleys used the park as a turn-around area and provided inexpensive transportation.

Roberson Museum and the Binghamton Visitor Center welcomes everyone to enjoy creative and interesting displays. A lovely mixed metal collage draws the attention of guests. All photos by Van Zandbergen Photography.

Changing times and private transportation allowing families to travel farther afield contributed to a gradual decline in local interest in the zoo, which almost closed in the early 1960s. In response, the Southern Tier Zoological Society was formed to rescue the zoo from its slow deterioration. Today the society manages the park, and among its many improvements are the creation of exhibits that closely resemble the animals' natural habitats, and a series of wooded pedestrian footpaths. The zoo is accredited by the American Association of Zoological Parks and Aquariums, testimony to the hard work and dedication of the zoo staff and all those who continue to work to maintain its high standards.

Today timber wolves and endangered red wolves roam the zoo's two-and-one-half-acre Wolf Woods, and Cat Country houses Siberian tigers, African lions, and a breathtaking rare white Bengal tiger. Visitors can observe a herd of big-horned mouflon sheep in a hillside exhibit, enjoy an unobstructed view

of endangered spectacled bears, or watch the antics of 18 black-footed penguins or a pair of African clawless otters that can be observed in their underwater habitat. The aviary is home to several species of birds. School children particularly enjoy visiting Valdessa, the first eagle rescued from the oil spill of the Exxon Valdez in 1989.

Ross Park Zoo also offers a variety of other educational opportunities, ranging from a Zoomobile that transports animals for on-site visits to a junior biologist program and, at Halloween, "haunted" animal exhibits at "Boo in the Zoo." Other fun programs are offered periodically throughout the year, and one can even get in shape at the zoo by taking advantage of a new exercise trail that winds among the animal exhibits. Funded by United Health Services, the hilly trail features periodic exercise stations and offers an easy way to combine environmental awareness with physical fitness.

The Discovery Center, also located at Ross Park, is a hands-on, interactive museum in which children can visit a model supermarket, "fly" a plane, or learn about dinosaurs or archaeology or how a telephone works. In 1995, the center welcomed a visit from poet Maya Angelou.

Families come to the Discovery Center ready to explore everything from painting to simple science projects. For 15 years the center has offered a variety of creative programs for preschoolers and parents, endearing itself to families with its acknowledgment that hands-on learning is not always a tidy proposition where preschoolers are concerned. Participants in many programs are invited to "dress for a mess," and the center promises to clean up afterward!

Roberson's Kopernik Space Education Center is a popular attraction in the area. It recently celebrated its 25th anniversary.

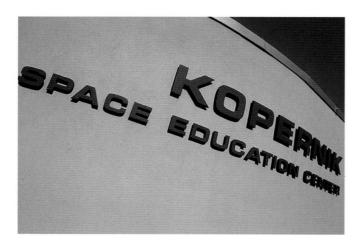

At its Binghamton campus in a Front Street mansion, the Roberson Museum and Science Center offers a variety of exhibitions, classes, and workshops. Formerly the home of the late Alonzo Roberson, Jr., and his wife, Margaret Hays Roberson, who bequeathed it for use as a cultural center following their deaths, the building was completed in 1907. Built in Italian Renaissance style by Binghamton architect Edward Vosbury, the mansion, with its elevator, dumbwaiter, central heating, and intercom system, had all the latest innovations of its day. Its third-floor billiard room now serves as a meeting room, and its ballroom is a gallery for changing exhibits. The Broome County Historical Society uses the elaborate second-floor master bedroom suite as exhibition space and maintains its library in the Robersons' first-floor library/living room.

For more than 40 years, Roberson Center has sponsored an annual Home for the Holidays celebration, one of its most popular events. Visitors enjoy displays celebrating Hanukkah and Ramadan, and stroll through an indoor forest of decorated trees. Eagerly awaited each year by children of all ages, the international Christmas forest showcases the holiday heritage of countries as diverse as Poland, Italy, Ukraine, and China, as well as the traditions

All photos by Van Zandbergen Photography.

Not all learning takes place in a classroom, of course, and Broome County offers ample opportunities to combine education with family fun.

Double columns at the door of Ridley Lowell Business School welcomes students each day.

of long-ago Christmases in the United States. Visitors also enjoy folk dancing, caroling, and a model train display. Ongoing programs in Roberson's Link Planetarium might include a look at star patterns at the winter solstice.

Throughout the year, Roberson offers a variety of programs that range from gatherings of model train aficionados to drawing and pottery classes or instruction in the Ukrainian folk art of pysanky. The intricate hand-decorating of eggs, incorporating the use of waxes and dyes to create meaningful patterns, pysanky is part of the heritage of many Broome County residents who today enjoy passing on this colorful tradition.

In 1997, Roberson received its first national grant for its YouthALIVE program, which targets teens who may need extra support through the adolescent years. Roberson provides young people with a safe environment in which to explore and learn. Many gain practical work experience by acting as assistants to the Roberson staff.

Today Roberson's education programs reach across New York State and Pennsylvania and serve 15 counties, 55 school districts, and 120 schools.

Roberson's Kopernik Space Education Center in Vestal offers young people from kindergarten through twelfth grade opportunities to explore the wonders of space, earth science, and technology. Whether one wishes to learn about model rocketry, consider close encounters, contemplate the meaning of black holes, study weather patterns, earthquakes, and global warming, or simply stargaze on a clear night, Kopernik can help point the way. For area students with a demonstrated interest in science, Kopernik's Science Talent Search offers total immersion programs in such subjects as astronomy, earth science, physics, and computer technology. Scholarships are available so that talented students from all walks of life can participate. The center's quality education programs in astronomy, space science, meteorology, computer imaging, geology, physics, and energy engineering have been recognized by the National Science Foundation and the New York State Department of Education.

Considered one of the best public observatories in the Northeast, the Kopernik Center celebrated its 25th anniversary in June 1999. Beginning in 1973, funds for its construction were raised by members of Broome County's active Polish-American

community, who wished to commemorate the 500th anniversary of the birth of Mikolaj Kopernik (Copernicus), the father of modern astronomy, in a way that would touch the lives of as many people as possible. With the help of other community groups and individuals from a variety of ethnic backgrounds, the Kopernik Center was dedicated a year later.

During the 1997-98 school year, 22,226 area students took advantage of programs at Roberson and Kopernik, which as a joint not-for-profit organization continues to rely on generous contributions from the community. Broome County's pride in and support of Kopernik has helped fund three observatory telescopes, a complete weather station, labs for the study of physics and lasers, space sciences, and computer imaging, a darkroom, an earthquake station, and a host of other site facilities.

A safe place to live and a long tradition of extending a warm welcome to newcomers. Extraordinary health-care facilities. Excellent schools and nationally ranked higher education institutions that make learning accessible for a lifetime, and ample opportunities to combine learning experiences with family fun. This is Broome County today as it focuses on its most important resource: the families who call it home. ■

Young writers have a relaxed learning experience in many of the schools. Photos by Van Zandbergen Photography.

Above: An archaeologist determines how to piece local treasures together. Photo by Van Zandbergen Photography.

Opposite page: A group of scientists study artifacts found in a recent archaeological dig.

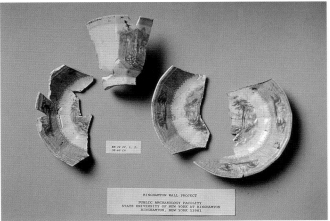

Left: Fragments of blue china have been mended near to its original state by archaeologists. Photos courtesy of Community Archaeology Program at Binghamton University.

The rowing team at Binghamton University requires many hours of training for the group of athletes. Photos courtesy of Binghamton University.

Smiling students is an encouraging sign that education continues to be a good experience in Broome County.

c h a p t e r

5

FOOD, FESTIVALS, AND FUN

Photo by Van Zandbergen Photography.

Previous page: Colorful balloons fill the night.

Above: Street vendors prepare foods for one of the many festivals in Broome County.

Opposite page: Colorful hot air balloons and good food are part of the Spiedies Festival. All photos by Van Zandbergen Photography.

The area has long abounded in restaurants serving the food of Italy and Eastern Europe, and over the years, newcomers have enriched the local dining scene with cuisine ranging from soul food, to Asian, French, seafood, and vegetarian specialities.

Many Broome County residents still recall the days when a Saturday night take-out dinner was a "hot pie," carried home in a twist of heavy white paper. Today hot pies are more commonly called pizzas, and cardboard boxes have replaced the paper wrappings. But one thing remains the same: The rich ethnic heritage of Broome County is reflected in its food, for all to enjoy. The area has long abounded in restaurants serving the food of Italy and Eastern Europe, and over the years, newcomers have enriched the local dining scene with cuisine ranging from soul food, to Asian, French, seafood, and vegetarian specialities.

As soon as Lent approaches each year, the congregations of the area's magnificent gold-domed Russian and Ukrainian churches don aprons to make dozens upon dozens of pierogies—squares of dough filled with potatoes or cheese—to fill phone orders that pour in from around the county. By 5 p.m., the church parking lots are filled with the cars of eager diners. Traditionally served piping hot with melted butter, pierogies make another appearance in summer when St. John's Ukrainian Church in Johnson City holds its annual Ukrainian Day. Kielbasi, another Eastern European specialty, is available year-round in many area restaurants and markets, some of which have developed special versions of the popular sausage for Easter and Thanksgiving.

But if there is one food that makes Broome County expatriates long for home, it is the spiedie. Tender, marinated chunks of lamb, chicken, or pork cooked on a skewer, spiedies appear on restaurant menus throughout the county, although locals agree they taste best when cooked outside on a grill. A few casual restaurants and taverns keep up an old tradition of grilling spiedies outside in good weather, where their tempting smell makes all but the most self-controlled passersby stop in their tracks. So devoted are current and former residents of Broome to their spiedies that marinade and skewers can now be found packaged for travel or mailing.

Spiedie lovers even have their own festival, held each summer at Tri-Cities Airport in Endicott. One of the most colorful and popular events of a Broome County summer, the Spiedie Fest and Balloon Rally treats festival-goers to the mouth-watering aromas of a spiedie cook-off and a rally of some 35 hot-air balloons. The cook-off has grown so popular that it now has three divisions: an open competition, for anyone with a great spiedie recipe; a celebrity contest in which local personalities show off their skills with a skewer; and a restaurant competition among local professional chefs.

More fun at Broome County festivals as residents prepare foods for the guests.

Opposite page: A beautiful Ferris wheel with the bright neon lights give an air of excitement as another festival begins. All photos by Van Zandbergen Photography.

Other festivals and fairs abound from spring through early fall, beginning with Windsor's Rhubarb Festival in May, and the annual Two Rivers Ethnic Festival at Broome County Veterans Memorial Arena, which celebrates the native foods, music, and dance of many countries. June brings the popular Greek Festival at the Greek Orthodox Church and Hellenic Center in Vestal. Here residents of all backgrounds feel transported to Greece for a day as they enjoy the beautiful setting and authentic food prepared by church members. Costumed dancers entertain, and lively music floats across the hills.

Deposit Days and Lumberjack Festival in July feature old-time competitions such as ax throwing and a Jack & Jill crosscut sawing competition, all in a homey, small-town atmosphere. The area's famous carousels are celebrated at an annual Carousel Festival in Endicott that attracts some 30 thousand visitors. Recent carousel celebrations have been enhanced by the showing of a documentary titled "Which Way EJ?," produced by Endicott native Brian Mauriello, that traces the early history of the Endicott-Johnson Corporation and its influence on Broome County. Also in July, downtown Binghamton hosts July Fest, a

colorful celebration of the visual and performing arts, and the Broome County Fair traditionally opens at the end of the month in Whitney Point.

In addition to the Spiedie Fest and Balloon Rally, August brings an Irish Festival featuring food, entertainment, and Irish dancing. The season begins to wind down in September when Johnson City hosts its annual Field Days. Area residents also enjoy the Jewish Ethnic Festival, a celebration of food, dance, and music held at the Jewish Community Center in Vestal. Octoberfest—celebration of food and fun named for the famous Munich Oktoberfest—is held in Kirkwood and is one of many activities sponsored throughout the year by the German Club. Endicott's annual Apple Fest, held in the Washington Avenue shopping district, helps round out the season.

These are but a few of the activities individuals and families can enjoy during the balmy months in Broome County. From Italian Feast Days to the annual June Pow Wow during which local Native Americans share their food, arts, music, and storytelling traditions, Broome County celebrates both the natural beauty and resources of the valley and the rich diversity of its citizens. ■

The Apple Cider Mill Festival brings out the excitement of many of the people as shown in the face of this youngster found in an apple bin. Photos by Van Zandbergen Photography.

Above: Produce glistens in a local market.

Right: A blueberry in a handmade basket invites the gourmet to take them home.

Opposite page: Antique cars are admired by all ages in Broome County. Photos by Van Zandbergen Photography

Everyone wants to be a part of the excitement in a Broome County festival. Parades are a regular part of celebrations in the area. Photos by Van Zandbergen Photography.

Residents of all backgrounds feel transported to Greece for a day as they enjoy the beautiful setting and authentic food prepared by church members. Costumed dancers entertain, and lively music floats across the hills.

THE PERFORMING ARTS

Photo by Stephen Appel, contributing photographer.

Previous page: Young thespians showcase Shakespeare's Work. All photos by Stephen Appel, contributing photographer.

Broome County residents have long been devoted supporters of the arts, enjoying music, theater, dance, and opera at venues throughout the area. Newcomers often express amazement at both the breadth and the quality of cultural life in Broome. Statistics compiled by the Broome County Arts Council give a succinct picture of the impact of the major cultural organizations: Together their combined annual operating expenditures exceed $4.6 million, 85 percent of which is spent within the county, and they employ more than 460 residents, including 42 in full-time positions.

One of Broome County's most beloved institutions, the Tri-Cities Opera (TCO) kicked off its 50th anniversary in fall 1998 by staging performances of *Kismet* and, over the holidays, its annual *Amahl and the Night Visitors*; these were followed in 1999 by *The Magic Flute* and *Madama Butterfly*, all at the Forum in Binghamton, an historic 1,500-seat performing arts center. Over the years, TCO has showcased numerous artists, many of whom, like Judy Berry, Cynthia Clarey, Jake Gardner, and Richard Leech, have gone on to major international careers.

When the opera company was founded by Peyton Hibbitt and the late Carmen Savoca, few could have anticipated the influence it would have on the music world half a century later. From TCO's inception in 1949 until his death in 1998, Savoca produced and/or stage-directed all but three of its productions, his credits including the world premieres of *Jeremiah*—in which he also sang the title role—as well as *Chinchilla* and *Galileo Galilei*.

For 50 years, Peyton Hibbitt served as artistic director, conductor, and music director, and was the vocal coach for the Resident Artist Training Program. Founder of the New York State Opera League, Hibbitt has conducted in Europe and throughout the United States. Like Savoca, he was for many years an adjunct professor and co-director of a program at Binghamton University that offers a master's degree in music with specialization in opera performance. In 1992, both men received a citation from New York Governor Mario Cuomo for their role in founding and developing TCO, and in 1993, they received the University Medal, one of the highest honors Binghamton University can bestow, from BU President Lois DeFleur.

Today Hibbitt continues his involvement with TCO as co-artistic director with Duane Skrabalak, who has been with TCO since 1970 as a singer, pianist, choral director, conductor, and voice coach, and who now serves as both artistic director and resident conductor.

The acting at local theaters include colorful costumes with perfect details.

With impressive directing and conducting credits in the United States and abroad, Skrabalak was hand-picked by TCO's co-founders as the person who could best lead the company into its second half-century and continue TCO's focus on the training of young singers. Skrabalak and Peter Sicilian, a 20 year TCO veteran and now its associate director and stage director, continue TCO's involvement with Binghamton University by serving as adjunct faculty members in BU's music department.

TCO's Resident Artist Training Program nurtures countless musicians from around the United States and Canada, and most recently from Eastern Europe. Many of them go on to professional careers as performers, teachers, and vocal coaches. Former students have appeared at the Metropolitan Opera in New York City, London's Covent Garden, La Scala in Milan, the Paris Opera, and the Deutsche Oper, the German Opera of Berlin. Many TCO graduates who choose to teach stay in the Broome County area, using their talents in local schools to train the next generation of musicians.

Local singers make up the chorus at most TCO productions, and volunteers help the opera in countless other ways, including serving on its board of directors and making generous donations during the annual fund-raising drives. TCO's two-year Million Dollar Campaign, announced in 1997, had reached the $900,000 mark by fall 1998. The money will be used to establish an endowment in honor of TCO's founders, provide a reserve fund, and continue the support of young singers into the new millennium.

Perhaps a quote from the Million Dollar Campaign brochure best summarizes the impact TCO has had on the world of opera: "After a European audition a few years ago, a distinguished conductor who was hearing the singers 'blind,' asked a singer whether he had ever sung at Tri-Cities Opera. When the astonished singer replied that he was indeed a TCO graduate, the conductor said he identified the vocalist's lyric beauty with the teaching techniques at TCO."

It is no wonder that former New York State Council on the Arts Chairwoman Kitty Carlisle Hart called TCO "the crown jewel of culture in the Southern Tier."

Broome County's only fully professional symphony orchestra, the Binghamton Philharmonic presents live classical and pops concerts to residents of Broome and surrounding counties under the leadership of Music Director John Covelli. A piano protege from age four, winner of major international piano competitions, and former teenage conductor of the elite Pierre Monteux master

Ballerinas wear replica clothing in each production. The graceful lines of a ballerina draws attention to the costumes as well as the performers. All photos by Stephen Appel, contributing photographer.

Broome County residents have long been devoted supporters of the arts, enjoying music, theater, dance, and opera at venues throughout the area.

The Binghamton Philharmonic provides many hours of relaxation for the area residents. Photo by Van Zandbergen Photography.

The string section of the Philharmonic must devote many hours to be a seasoned performer.

class, Maestro Covelli's musical accomplishments span the worlds of orchestral and chamber music, opera, ballet, Broadway, recordings, and arranging, as well as the multifaceted world of symphonic pops.

Formed in July 1996, as the result of a merger between the Binghamton Symphony and Choral Society and the BC Pops, the Philharmonic has achieved a level of artistic excellence unusual for a regional orchestra. Made up principally of fine musicians from Greater Binghamton, the Philharmonic's challenging repertory also attracts musicians from upstate New York, Pennsylvania, and New York City. In addition to playing the great masterworks of composers such as Beethoven, Mahler, Strauss, and Sibelius, the orchestra has maintained a special commitment to the music of contemporary Americans and has commissioned several new works from composers with ties to the Broome County area. The orchestra's classical concerts feature internationally renowned guest artists as well as important emerging soloists. The musical achievements of the Binghamton Philharmonic have been recognized by grants from the New York State Council on the Arts and by local and national foundations.

Each season the Philharmonic Pops presents a series of entertaining concerts featuring guest artists from the worlds of jazz, Broadway, and entertainment, as well as popular classical "crossover" artists. The Philharmonic's annual family-oriented Holiday Festival of Music, which features area school choruses, the Binghamton Youth Symphony, and amateur and professional ice skaters, has become a holiday tradition.

In addition, the Philharmonic's educational programs help introduce younger generations to the joys of making and listening to music. The orchestra's annual Young People's Concerts entertain and educate some three thousand schoolchildren each year. The Philharmonic also provides an innovative in-school, curriculum-based music appreciation program for preschoolers and children through second grade, and provides ensemble groups to area schools for performances and master classes.

Theater lovers need not travel to New York City or elsewhere. Each year, at the Forum in Binghamton, the Broadway Theatre League presents nationally touring Broadway shows ranging from *Guys and Dolls* and *Oklahoma*, to *Oliver* and *A Chorus Line*.

Since 1976 drama lovers have enjoyed professional theater at the Cider Mill Playhouse in Endicott. Inside the warehouse of a functioning cider mill, the 274-seat theater is designed cabaret-style, with seating on risers. Sight lines are excellent throughout, and the playhouse's thrust stage allows the action to take place practically in the midst of the audience.

Originally founded by the Theater Department at Binghamton University, in 1991 the theater was incorporated as a freestanding nonprofit organization with a mission "to provide affordable professional drama to local residents, thereby stimulating an interest in the main issues addressed by drama as well as in drama as an art form." The only professional drama group in the region, the playhouse stages seven diverse productions a year. Suitable productions often have special showings for school-age children during the school day, with post-performance discussions led by the actors as a way of enhancing the educational experience. The playhouse's annual production of *A Christmas Carol* has become a popular holiday tradition for many Broome County families.

World-class performances in music and dance take place at Binghamton University's Anderson Center. At 91,465 square feet, the area's largest theater complex showcases music, dance, and drama from around the world in its three theaters and outdoor amphitheater. Past performers have included the Central Ballet of China, who in 1986 made the Anderson Center the first stop on its first North American tour; other U.S. premieres have included Lezginka, the State Ensemble of Folk Dance of Daghesta, in the

The conductor spends many hours with his artists to plan the perfect performance. Photos by Van Zandbergen Photography.

former USSR, and the Berlin Symphony Philharmonic in 1987. Among other notable performances have been those of the Pittsburgh Symphony, the Alvin Ailey American Dance Theater, the Juilliard String Quartet, and world-renowned musicians such as classical guitarist Christopher Parkening and cellist Lynn Harrell. The 1998-99 season included performances by the New York City Ballet during its 50th-anniversary season, the St. Petersburg Symphony Orchestra, the Russian National Ballet, and the New York Philharmonic.

Above & Below: **A circle of children watches intently as they receive a spellbinding story by their teacher.**

Opposite page: **Teachers exchange ideas as they prepare for their jobs. All photos by Van Zandbergen Photography.**

In keeping with its global focus, the Anderson Center has hosted two major international festivals—a Northern Ireland festival in 1992, and a Scottish festival in 1996, both in collaboration with the British Council. A Greek festival is planned for 1999-2000.

Ever since the Anderson Center's completion in 1985, the Binghamton Summer Music Festival has taken advantage of its facilities to host performances in July and August by entertainment luminaries as diverse as Pearl Bailey, the Israel Philharmonic with Zubin Mehta, Wynton Marsalis, Rudolf Nureyev, Tony Bennett, Dionne Warwick, Natalie Cole, and Glenn Campbell, as well as free music events each summer at venues throughout the county. The festival is supported by an approximately 200-member Festival Circle of music-loving residents and area businesses who work toward a common goal of bringing the sound of music and the joy of dance to Broome County throughout the summer.

Plays by students in Binghamton University's nationally known theater department are also frequently performed at the Anderson Center and attract an enthusiastic audience from well beyond the campus.

Area residents also take advantage of drama, dance, and musical performances offered by Theatre/BCC and the Jazz Ensemble, Flute Ensemble, and College Choir at Broome Community College. Many nationally known performers, including Chuck Mangione, Maynard Ferguson, Richie Havens, the Count Basie Orchestra, and the Artie Shaw Orchestra, have come to the BCC campus, which has also hosted productions by the National Shakespeare Company.

Recognizing the importance of introducing children to the arts, the Southern Tier Institute for Arts in Education administers programs to provide arts-centered learning for students and to train teachers in ways of using the arts within the curriculum. Among these is Wolf Trap Early Learning Through the Arts, a program of the international Wolf Trap Foundation for the Performing Arts, headquartered in Vienna, Virginia, which exposes pre-kindergarten students to creative dramatics, storytelling, puppetry, music, and dance, presented during residencies by professional artists trained to work with children. The Aesthetic Education Institute for grades K–12 provides similar age-appropriate opportunities for school-age children. Two-week summer programs help introduce teachers to new and creative ways of presenting the arts to their students.

The arts flourish in Broome County, attracting audiences from all walks of life—from preschoolers enchanted by their first live stage performance, to adults eager for an evening's professional entertainment, to family members of all ages who play vital roles in the arts scene as volunteers and enthusiastic supporters. ■

Students perform in the local theatre productions. Photo courtesy of Binghamton University.

Gladys Knight's performance was a showstopper for everyone who chose to take an evening to reminisce to her popular love songs. Photo by Van Zandbergen Photography.

The arts flourish in Broome County, attracting audiences from all walks of life—from preschoolers enchanted by their first live stage performance, to adults eager for an evening's professional entertainment, to family members of all ages who play vital roles in the arts scene as volunteers and enthusiastic supporters.

chapter

HELPING HANDS

Photo by Van Zandbergen Photography.

Previous page: Colorful fireworks displays all the excitement at First Night, an annual New Years Party in Broome County.

Above: Volunteers and local not-for-profit organizations are supported by various funding sources, including government and business. Photos by Van Zandbergen Photography.

A vital community is much more than its geography and economy. Community service programs and organizations form a network and support system that is often overlooked—yet these very services may be deciding factors in whether a prospective employee moves to the area, an established family decides to stay, or a recent college graduate returns to pursue a career and start a family.

Volunteers are the lifeblood of many Broome County human-service organizations. Individuals and families from all walks of life lift a hammer for Habitat for Humanity, deliver friendship as well as nourishing food for Meals on Wheels, hold the hands and ease the hearts of the dying, transport the elderly to medical appointments, and show in countless other ways that they care about each other and the community they call home. Recently, concerned individuals from a wide range of professional backgrounds voluntarily formed a steering committee to study the effects of welfare reform in Broome County and to make appropriate recommendations.

Local not-for-profit organizations are supported by various funding sources, including government and business, as well as

individual donors. In addition, Broome County charitable foundations, which run the gamut from small family foundations to the Hoyt Foundation and the Greater Broome Community Foundation, often provide the means for programs to be initiated and buildings to be constructed, as well as assisting not-for-profit groups in times of crisis.

Since 1970, the private Hoyt Foundation, established as a legacy of the late Port Dickinson native Willma Hoyt after her husband Stewart's death, has disbursed over $10 million to large and small not-for-profit agencies in Broome County. The Greater Broome Community Foundation was established in 1997 as a public charity by a group of caring citizens as a means of expanding philanthropy in Broome and surrounding counties. Through the foundation's general fund, or by establishing advised funds, philanthropic citizens made it possible for the foundation to grant a total of $101,000 to 21 local organizations in fall 1998. In addition to disbursing grants, both foundations provide technical assistance to not-for-profit agencies, serve as informal clearinghouses, and convene community forums.

Local human-service organizations have long tried to meet both immediate and long-term needs of Broome County residents, particularly children, the elderly, and lower-income families. Child-care resources include facilities like Mom's House, whose sites in Endicott and Binghamton provide free, quality child care and related services for low-income, single parents in

Volunteers are the lifeblood of many Broome County human-service organizations. Individuals and families from all walks of life show in countless ways that they care about each other and the community they call home.

Photos by Van Zandbergen Photography.

exchange for a commitment to work three hours at the center each week, attend school regularly and maintain passing grades, and donate a few hours of fund-raising time.

The Broome County Child Development Council (BCCDC) Corner-Copia Resource Room in Binghamton lends toys and videos to day-care providers and produces a quarterly newsletter of child-care tips, nutritional information, and activity ideas. Also located in Binghamton, as well as in Endicott, Johnson City, and Chenango Forks, four Parent Resource Centers, a joint venture of Cornell Cooperative Extension of Broome County and the Mothers & Babies Perinatal Network, promote family self-sufficiency by sponsoring parenting classes, lending educational materials and children's literature, and providing on-site health and developmental screening.

Other social services aid a cross-section of Broome County residents. The Southern Tier Independence Center fosters independent living for people with disabilities by offering a wide range of services that may include locating readers and sign-language interpreters, sponsoring workshops on independent living skills, assisting with housing needs, or lending equipment. The Broome County Council of Churches' Neighborhood Interfaith Volunteer Caregiver Program assists the elderly or disabled with daily tasks, provides transportation for shopping and appointments, and offers respite for full-time caregivers. Local places of worship serve as clearinghouses to identify individuals in need of assistance, train volunteers, and raise funds to support various programs.

Located in one of Binghamton's oldest neighborhoods, the First Ward Action Council is an innovative organization that loans tools, provides free or low-cost home repair to low-income residents over age 55, and purchases and renovates older buildings into attractive storefronts and affordable apartments.

The Crime Victims Assistance Center in Binghamton provides victim advocacy from the time a crime is reported and throughout the criminal justice process. The center sponsors Victims Rights Week and a conference on family violence, and advocates for child welfare.

ACCORD, a center for dispute resolution, is an umbrella organization for programs promoting peaceful conflict resolution, including CASA, representing children in Family Court; PEACE, a group counseling program for young men with a history of violent or aggressive behavior; and the Community Mediation Project, which recruits and trains volunteer mediators for cases referred by courts and law enforcement agencies.

Citizens are involved in a local walkathon as they show concern for health issues. Photos by Van Zandbergen Photography.

Other not-for-profit agencies provide vital information, among them Care and Consequences, a collaborative project of Four County Library, United Health Services, and WSKG Public Broadcasting that both publicizes and provides forums for discussion of end-of-life issues.

Still others, such as Binghamton First Night, focus on family-oriented events. The annual New Year's Eve celebration begun in 1996, which draws up to 14 thousand people to an alcohol-free party and arts performances in downtown Binghamton, results from the work of 150 year-round volunteers and some eight hundred who contribute their time on First Night. RiverQuest, sponsored in the spring by Imagination Celebration, is a multidimensional festival that explores connections among artistic, cultural, and scientific disciplines.

Both large and small arts groups within Broome County depend for much of their success on community volunteers who perceive a need and contribute their time and talents. Like many other not-for-profit groups, the Community Music Center was begun as the

vision of a local resident. Today its sites in Binghamton and Endicott make professionally taught music lessons available on a sliding scale to students who might not otherwise be able to afford them.

The Deposit Community Theatre and Performing Arts Center, located in the town's historic State Theatre, brings film, theater, music, and dance to rural eastern Broome County. Theatricks by Starlight, the "playhouse in residence" at the theater, puts on several different performances a year, providing entertainment at affordable prices and offering an outlet for local talent.

These are but a sample of the not-for-profit agencies that enhance life for all Broome County citizens. They represent what is best about Broome County today—the caring people who donate their time and energy to make it a friendly, supportive community for all.

This chapter is sponsored by the Hoyt Foundation, which, together with the Greater Broome Community Foundation, is privileged to know first hand the work done by volunteers throughout the community. ■

The help of volunteers is evident throughout the area. Photos by Van Zandbergen Photography.

These not-for-profit agencies enhance life for all
Broome County citizens. They represent what is
best about Broome County today—the caring
people who donate their time and energy to make
it a friendly, supportive community for all.

Food banks are a great way to show concern for Broome County as well as a way for neighbors to fellowship with one another. Photos by Van Zandbergen Photography.

The support of residents of Broome County has played a positive part of keeping our citizens happy and content to live here. Photos by Van Zandbergen Photography.

A vital community is much more than its geography and economy. Community service programs and organizations form a network and support system that is often overlooked—yet these very services may be deciding factors in whether a prospective employee moves to the area, an established family decides to stay, or a recent college graduate returns to pursue a career and start a family.

c h a p t e r

LOOKING TO THE FUTURE

Photo by Van Zandbergen Photography.

From its location at the confluence of two historic rivers to its mix of charming villages, townships, and city amenities, today's Broome County is an attractive area in which to establish a home, raise a family, or locate a business. Its central location makes it ideal — key highway interchanges provide easy access to the entire Northeast and Canada, and Broome's bustling Binghamton Regional Airport, conveniently located just seven miles north of the city, offers excellent connections for business travelers. Local commutes to work average less than 20 minutes each way over well-maintained and often scenic roads.

Among the area's most appealing qualities to employers is the well established work ethic of its labor pool — stable, loyal, and ranked 27 percent more productive than the national average. Many long-time residents today are the descendants of the first workers at Endicott-Johnson, IBM, and other area industries, who have the same can-do attitude as those who came before them; still others are newer residents of the area from around the country and around the world, bringing with them diverse backgrounds and skills that enhance both the workplace and the wider community.

Photos by Van Zandbergen Photography.

Broome County is still home to a major IBM facility; with some 5,500 employees, the data processing giant remains the county's largest employer. Other large technology industries include Lockheed Martin, with facilities in both Broome and Tioga counties, and Universal Instruments. These, and the area's numerous mid-size and small technology firms, make Broome County the home of the third strongest concentration of high-tech industries in the United States. As it looks to the future, Broome County will continue to attract some of the finest technological minds in the country to the peaceful valley that has such a well-deserved reputation for innovation and excellence.

Numerous initiatives, many of them collaborations among established Broome County businesses, area higher education facilities, and local government, promote the growth of new business in the area, with emphasis on entrepreneurship and small business start-up. From Partnership 2000, which launched a $2.3 million "Getting it Done" campaign to help fund local job creation, to the nonprofit Broome County Economic Development Alliance, new businesses can take advantage of a wide range of services ranging from needs assessment to government interface.

To encourage the growth of smaller businesses in the area, a State Senate initiative called ExCEL was recently established. Sponsored by Senator Thomas Libous, and administered through Broome Community College with the goal of helping the area continue its rebound from the big-industry downsizing of the

From its location at the confluence of two historic rivers to its mix of charming villages, townships, and city amenities, today's Broome County is an attractive area in which to establish a home, raise a family, or locate a business.

The family of IBM has been a constant force within the professional community. Photo courtesy of IBM.

early 1990s, ExCEL assists both new and existing small businesses through professional consultations and the establishment of business, tax, financing, insurance, and other training programs for entrepreneurs.

Binghamton University's Small Business Development Center and Trade Adjustment Assistance Center have a long tradition of working closely with area business professionals and local entrepreneurs, offering a wide range of programs tailored to the needs of both existing and potential businesses.

Citizens of Broome County, whether they pursue careers in large, high-tech industries, education, health services, retail, or one of the small to midsize businesses springing up throughout the area, enjoy a quality of life remarkable enough to have received national acclaim. For example, Binghamton, the Broome County seat, has been a finalist for the City Livability Award given by the U.S. Conference of Mayors.

In addition, in a study of more than 140 metropolitan areas throughout the United States, Cleveland State University researchers named the Binghamton area the best choice for those concerned with the quality of community life. *Money* magazine has rated the Binghamton area as high as 20th out of 300 similar-size metropolitan areas as the best place to live, and a three-year study by the University of Kentucky ranked Broome sixth of 253 urban counties nationwide as having the highest quality of life, making it the highest-ranking New York county.

The low crime rate, below-U.S.-average cost of buying a single-family home, ready access to excellent educational facilities and health care, burgeoning arts community, and above all the dedication of citizens committed to making the area inclusive, warm, and welcoming, make Broome County, on the cusp of the new millennium, a most attractive place in which to live. ■

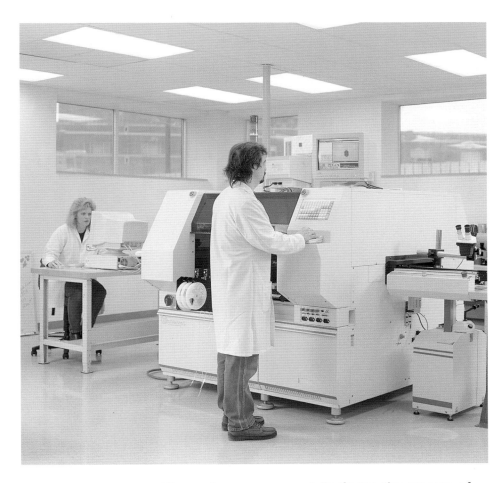

Men and women are contributing to the success of the technical age we are now experiencing in Broome County.

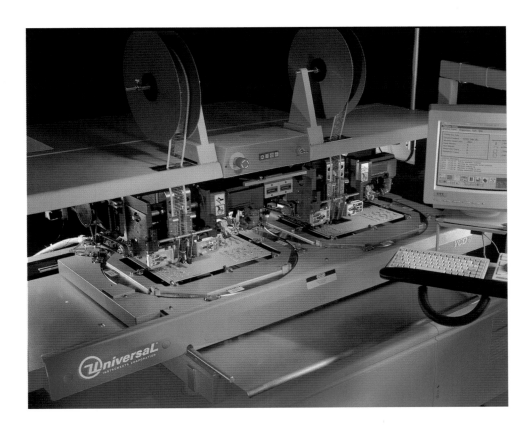

Above: Elected officials tour Broome County.
Right: The beauty of the fall foliage contributes to a picture-perfect work environment. The outdoor area is a favorite place to find workers during their lunch breaks.

Construction is a constant reminder of the ever-changing world in Broome County. Photos by Van Zandbergen Photography.

Photos by Van Zandbergen Photography.

The low crime rate, below-U.S.-average cost of buying a single-family home, ready access to excellent educational facilities and health care, burgeoning arts community, and above all the dedication of citizens committed to making the area inclusive, warm, and welcoming, make Broome County, on the cusp of the new millennium, a most attractive place in which to live.

2

BROOME
COUNTY
ENTERPRISES

Photo by Van Zandbergen Photography.

c h a p t e r

MANUFACTURING

National Pipe & Plastics, Inc.

Name recognition for manufacturing companies in the central New York region often gets buried under such giants as IBM and Corning. Yet many manufacturers, so vital to the local economies, provide the underlying stability which supports the communities during the cyclical employment swings of these corporate giants.

One such manufacturer, National Pipe & Plastics, Inc., 3241 Old Vestal Road, has endured the ups and downs of the local economy without layoffs, cutbacks, or diminished production. National began producing pipe in June of 1970. Since that time its facility has grown from 45,000 square feet to 147,000 square feet, its production capacity has doubled, and its employment levels have increased steadily.

Today, National employs 181 people in Broome County, its corporate headquarters, and an additional 97 people in its North Carolina facility.

"National produces over 220 million pounds of pipe a year, is the 10th largest pipe producer in America, and the 14th largest employer in Broome County," says Chuck Miller, vice president of manufacturing. Its Vestal facility, which has been operating for 28 years, has many employees with over 25 years of service, a strong testimony to the importance of National.

"Local citizens driving down Old Vestal Road to the UPS turnoff at Commerce Road will see our blue, gray, purple, green, and white pipe stacked in the yard ready for shipment," says Verne Clair, vice president of operations. "We ship 20 to 25 truckloads of pipe from this yard every day."

"Our pipe is shipped throughout the eastern seaboard," says Mark Cuda, vice president of sales, "from Maine to Florida, from the East Coast to Illinois, Kentucky, Tennessee, and Alabama, and into Canada."

The production of PVC pipe evolved during the 1920s along with the development of a multitude of plastic products for home and industry. This durable plastic pipe quickly gained acceptance

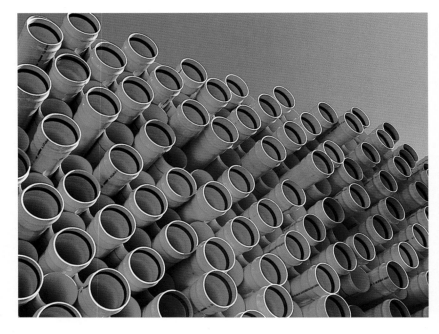

National manufactures pipe ranging in size from the tiny half-inch diameter to the immense 24-inch diameter with applications in the water, sewer, plumbing, and electrical industries. Photo by Carriage House Photography.

around the world, proving to be clean, durable, fire resistant, easy to ship, and easy to install, as well as impervious to rust, rodents, termites, and corrosive soils.

PVC (polyvinyl chloride) is a virtually indestructible plastic resistant to many chemicals, corrosion, and contaminates. Since its development PVC has revolutionized the pipe industry, eliminating rust and corrosion problems associated with more traditional iron pipe.

National manufactures pipe ranging in size from the tiny half-inch diameter to the immense 24-inch diameter with applications in the water, sewer, plumbing, and electrical industries. Telephone companies use PVC pipe to protect their underground telephone lines. Electricians use PVC conduit to shield their electrical wiring. Golf enthusiasts reap the benefits of PVC pipe used to irrigate golf courses. Municipalities across the nation depend on PVC pipe to provide clean, pure drinking water to their citizens, as well as to maintain a continuous free flow of water through their vital sewer systems.

It was 1869 when a printer in Albany, New York, named John W. Hyatt, seeking a substitute for ivory to make billiard balls, invented celluloid, the first synthetic plastic. Since that time plastics have been continuously improved to serve our needs and improve our quality of life. Today, plastic is an integral part of the modern world used in everything from heart valves to picnic products, from artificial limbs to lawn furniture, from children's playground equipment to PVC pipe.

National Pipe & Plastics' corporate office is located on Old Vestal Road in Vestal, New York. Photo by Carriage House Photography.

"Billions of pounds of vinyl are produced in the United States every year," says J. Allan McLean, president and CEO of National Pipe. "Vinyl is everywhere because of its cost-efficiency and environmental performance. We here at National," he says, "are only a small part of the worldwide plastics community."

And as part of this plastic community, National is committed to producing a quality product. The pipe produced at National meets standards for UL (Underwriter's Laboratories), NSF (National Sanitation Foundation), ASTM (American Society for Testing Materials), CSA (Canadian Standards Association), and AWWA (American Water Works Association). "But we're not just about pipe," says Allan McLean; "we're about our people and we're about Broome County."

National involves itself in local fund-raising events and makes regular contributions to civic charities, acknowledging its corporate responsibility to the community. The spirit of teamwork at National extends beyond the workplace: a company softball team, summer picnics, a yearly dinner dance, the children's Christmas party, golf tournaments, a cook-out where managers put on chef hats and cook lunch for the employees. "Here at National," says Dave Culbertson, treasurer and CFO, "we're not just growing as a business; we're growing as a family."

The company newsletter ties them together, reporting pipe news, recounting all the printable gossip, congratulating individuals on exemplary performance, offering discount coupons, providing information about educational assistance and other

PVC (polyvinyl chloride) is a virtually indestructible plastic resistant to many chemicals, corrosion, and contaminates. Pictured here is the high output PVC pipe extrusion line in Vestal. Photo by Carriage House Photography.

company benefits, and keeping track of the latest births, marriages, anniversaries, and birthdays.

All these things contribute to the success of a dynamic company committed to the future. "We are proud of our company, the dedication and focus of our employees," says Allan McLean, "and we are proud to be a part of Broome County, which has supported National in its continued growth. This Broome County and local area support has come in many forms—cost improvement research, workforce training, traffic planning, product research, and continuing education programs, to name a few." ■

The Vestal finished pipe yard ships approximately 130 million pounds of PVC pipe annually, or 20 to 25 truckloads a day.

The Raymond Corporation

From Syracuse to Singapore and Copehagen to Cape Town, The Raymond Corporation is a legendary world leader in the highly competitive materials handling industry.

Raymond's worldwide lift truck manufacturing presence includes facilities in New York, Iowa, Canada, and Sweden. Nine out of 10 *Fortune 100* companies use Raymond's products. Four out of five operators use—and win with—Raymond's vehicles in national lift truck competitions. More than two-thirds of all Raymond® lift trucks built over the last 30 years are still in service today, moving loads, saving space, and saving time.

Customers enjoy the support of the strongest independent dealer network of its kind. The Raymond Dealer Network provides warehouse design assistance, technical service, training, rental equipment, and financing packages. These consultative professionals consistently create the most productive and cost-efficient solutions to answer today's materials handling challenges.

For over a century the village of Greene, New York, has been the home of The Raymond Corporation. It had its beginnings in 1840, when the Lyon Iron Works was founded, producing cast iron agricultural tools. Many of Lyon's early American farming implements are now on exhibit at the Farmer's Museum in Cooperstown, New York.

By the early 1900s the iron works was struggling in a rapidly changing, industrialized economy. In 1922, George G. Raymond Sr., an industrial engineer from Brooklyn, purchased control of the foundry and led the company into the burgeoning materials handling market.

Over the decades that followed, the company introduced a string of innovative products that literally changed the way the world moves materials.

In 1928, the company introduced the first hydraulic hand pallet truck. Shortly after World War II, its revolutionary *Space-Saver* brand straddle truck helped create greater storage density within a warehouse. This slim, battery-powered forklift

Raymond's best-selling Reach-Fork® trucks are high-tech descendants of its early Space-Saver® straddle truck first introduced in 1950.

Operators of the Swing-Reach® truck by Raymond enjoy single-handed control of numerous functions. A former jet fighter pilot designed Raymond's handle.

moved and turned in tight quarters, permitting racks to be installed closer together. And so was born the modern "narrow aisle" lift truck industry.

Through the '50s, '60s, and '70s, The Raymond Corporation continued to develop innovative mechanical products—while integrating the machines with emerging technologies. Wire guidance systems made it easier for operators to navigate increasingly narrower aisles. Raymond's philosophy of continuous improvement inspired a regular flow of mechanical, electrical, and electronic design patents.

Then in the late 1980s, The Raymond Corporation undertook several dramatic initiatives. The company integrated microprocessor technology into its products, modernizing its facilities to achieve world-class production standards. As a result, Raymond has enjoyed record growth throughout the 1990s.

In 1997, this profitable, stable manufacturer attracted a buyer, BT Industries AB of Sweden. Successfully paired with an equally accomplished European materials handling manufacturer, the two organizations now command a leading share of the world's warehouse lift truck market. Combining the companies served to strengthen their respective market positions in Europe and North America—while supporting continued expansion into other emerging markets.

Today, innovations such as the company's new series of *Millennium*™ lift trucks position Raymond for leadership into the next century. Further leveraging Raymond's materials handling focus and strong distribution channels, its fast-growing subsidiary, Dockstocker Corporation, pursues the dock-to-stock vehicle market with its own line of reliable, efficient, electric lift trucks. Meanwhile, other innovative programs and products continue to bolster Raymond's competitiveness and value on behalf of its customers and the entire BT Industries family of companies. ∎

Frito-Lay, Inc.

The year 1999 marks the 25th anniversary of Frito-Lay in Broome County, but the successful snack food industry began in 1932 when Elmer Doolin produced Frito brand corn chips. In 1938 Herman W. Lay purchased an Atlanta potato chip company, changing the name to H. W. Lay & Co., and in 1961 the two merged to become Frito-Lay. A 1965 merger with the Pepsi-Cola Corporation formed a new company, Pepsico.

Currently, approximately 600,000 pounds of corn and over 20 million pounds of potatoes are used each week. Using only the highest quality fresh produce, over 90 million pounds of snack food is manufactured here annually. Over 1.5 million bags are filled each day, equal to about six tons per hour. The plant makes over 200 different line items at the Kirkwood facility, with numerous sizes and seasonings, including Lays and Ruffles brand potato chips, Frito brand corn chips, Doritos, Tostitos, and Santitas brand tortilla chips, Munchos brand potato chips, and Real Restaurant Style Tortilla Chips, all instantly recognizable to consumers worldwide. The local warehouse facility moves at least 500,000 cases of chips every week, with the traffic center dispatching more than 40 trailers each day to various locations in New York, New Jersey, Pennsylvania, and the mid-Atlantic areas.

Using only the highest quality fresh produce, over 90 million pounds of snack food is manufactured at the Kirkwood facility annually. Photo by Carriage House Photography.

When the Kirkwood plant opened in 1974, it employed 120 people, and today the number has grown to 700. Forty of the current staff were among the original number hired. Loyalty and friendliness are hallmarks of the dedicated team of today's employees, and many aspects of the business depend on employee involvement in day-to-day operational decisions. It is a team effort that has allowed the Kirkwood site to be recognized nationally as a leader in service to its customers. These same people also show support for the community by participating in events such as the American Cancer Society's Relay for Life and Making Strides Against Breast Cancer. They additionally contribute time and funds annually to the United Way Campaign and many other worthwhile projects and events.

Recognizing the importance of maintaining a healthy environment, the corporation has created an impressive in-house Green Team responsible for overseeing the effective reuse of industry by-products. Among the many uses for the nutrient-rich waste are starch and animal food.

Frito-Lay's growth potential is unlimited, as the demand for high quality snack food continues to increase throughout the world. ■

The Kirkwood plant employs 700 people. Loyalty and friendliness are hallmarks of the dedicated team of today's employees, and many aspects of the business depend on employee involvement in day-to-day operational decisions. It is a team effort that has allowed the Kirkwood site to be recognized nationally as a leader in service to its customers. Photo by Carriage House Photography.

Doron Precision Systems, Inc.

In 1973 a world leader was born—Doron Precision Systems, Inc. A quarter of a century ago Carl Wenzinger and partners saw the possibilities the future could hold for driving and entertainment simulation systems. The distinct dual product lines ensure the company's future in global markets.

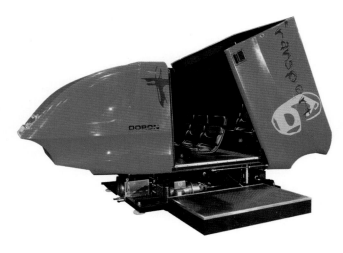

Doron was the first company in the entertainment simulation market. Transport 6 is a Doron entertainment simulator.

The first step was the acquisition of the Singer LINK driving simulation hardware business. In 1974, this was enlarged by incorporating the entire driving simulation film library from the Allstate Insurance Company. This made Doron the first organization to offer complete driving simulation systems, including development and production of the hardware, audiovisual software, and computer software subsystems.

Today, Doron owns the world's most comprehensive library of copyrighted driving simulation film and laser videodisc programs for land vehicle driver instruction. The use of these state-of-the-art simulation systems facilitates the teaching, testing, and screening of basic procedural and perceptual driving skills in the controlled environment of the simulator classroom, saving fuel and making roads safer for everyone.

Doron was the first company in the entertainment simulation market. There are now hundreds of Doron entertainment simulators in over 60 different countries. The Doron idea of entertainment simulation was years ahead of its time. It took a lot of effort, development, and marketing to create today's success story.

Every Doron entertainment simulator is engineered and manufactured in Doron's 100,000-square-foot facility to exacting specifications which assure safety, comfort, and enjoyable experiences. The simulators create a stirring auditory, visual, and tactile experience, making every experience more realistic and thrilling. Sight, sound, wind, and motion are blended to bring a high level of reality to participants immersed in encounters exciting the senses.

Because Doron designs and manufactures its own products, it controls every element in the simulators and can easily customize to meet any requirements. The experience Doron has gained from the installation of hundreds of entertainment simulators around the world is a key advantage for the museums, tourist attractions, parks, and educational institutions benefiting from Doron's vision and commitment.

Options are endless, from helicopters and race cars to trips through the body, or a journey through the electronics inside a computer. Dozens of unique and educational applications are being created on a regular basis, but only programs that meet high standards for family entertainment are developed. One of the newest is an underwater exploratory vehicle that allows students an unparalleled marine biology experience—right in the classroom. The innovative learning mode combines the basic sciences for experiments in an underwater setting.

Since the company's inception it has adhered to conservative ideals, with a policy of investing in development, exemplary service, progress, and excellence—all made possible by the corporate philosophy of faith in the employees who produce the simulation systems and the clients who purchase the products. As simulation technology advances, Doron of Broome County will continue to train and test on a global scale, and make life more entertaining. ∎

Doron was the first organization to offer complete driving simulation systems, including development and production of the hardware, audiovisual software, and computer software subsystems. Amos II is a Doron driving simulator.

Dovatron International, Inc.

Established in 1970 as the contract manufacturing arm of Universal Instruments (a subsidiary of Dover Corporation), Dovatron International, Binghamton, New York, division, has the distinction of being the flagship of the Dii Group. Over the years the branch grew, and in 1993 spun off completely from Dover Corporation as a public company headquartered in Colorado.

Today, as part of the Dii Group, Dovatron International has five uniquely linked sister companies—Dii Semiconductor, Dii Technologies Design, Multek, Dii Interconnect, and Dii Technologies Test. This group of linked companies provides a broad range of services from concept design to prototypes to volume assembly, box build, distribution, and total life cycle management. The Dii Group has established Technology Centers, such as the one in Binghamton, to provide the knowledge, technology, expertise, and strategic worldwide locations to help customers penetrate global markets. These services are continually improved with ongoing investments in cutting-edge technology to ensure that all Dii business units remain up-to-date and state-of-the-art.

An industry leader since 1970, the Dovatron New York division ably serves customers in the mid-Atlantic, mid-America, and New England from the heart of Broome County. The New York facility, located in the Broome Corporate Park, currently covers 110,000 square feet, with plentiful expansion options. Highly trained individuals staff the Broome operation, where employee involvement is promoted at all levels. Continuous training ensures quality and improved output. Dovatron's service-oriented organization is built on the talents and experience of its innovative staff, and Dovatron's management further believes that supporting community charities, educational institutions, arts, and social events is all part of being a good corporate neighbor.

As a top tier, world-class contract electronics manufacturer,

Dovatron's 110,000-square-foot facility is located in Broome Industrial Park, Conklin, New York.

Dovatron International has the financial strength and resources required for ongoing investment in equipment, personnel, and services to meet the growing demands of global clients. With worldwide facilities strategically located in the Americas, Europe, and Asia, it is Dovatron's goal not only to build long-term relationships with customers, but also to be an essential contributor to their continued success. ∎

Fully automated assembly lines are capable of supporting traditional assembly technology and advanced technology applications.

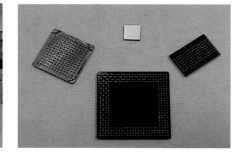

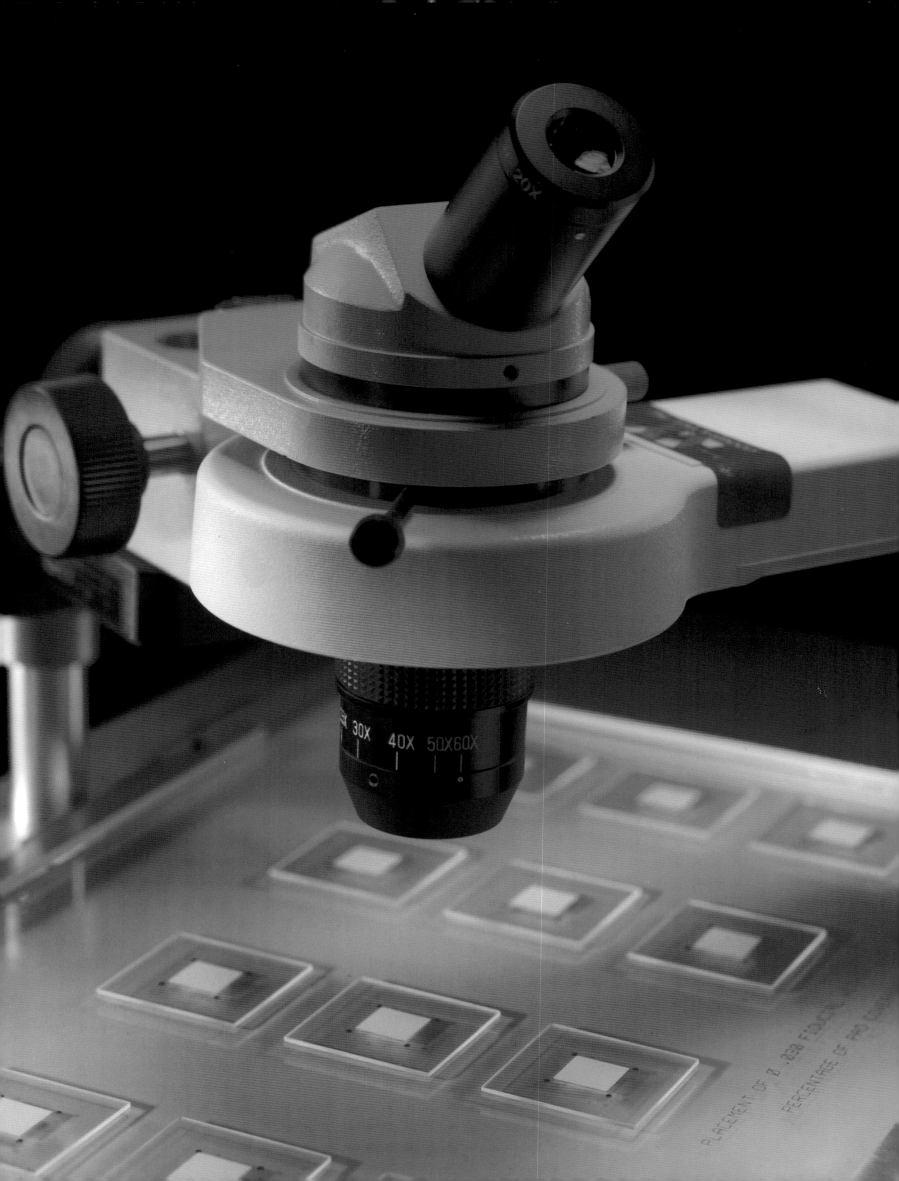

c h a p t e r

HIGH-TECH

IBM Endicott

ith roots tracing back to the early 1900s, Endicott proudly carries the title "Birthplace of IBM." From its modest beginnings until today, IBM Endicott's history is rich with technological developments and product leadership. Currently a producer of electronics packaging technology and software, and a provider of e-business and engineering solutions, Endicott carries out a wide variety of service and state-of-the-art product missions serving other IBM locations and external customers.

As the company's original location, IBM Endicott's history is long and colorful. Yet it sprang from humble beginnings. The year was 1911 when IBM began its corporate life in a small lumbering village along the Susquehanna River known as Endicott. That year, three small firms that manufactured food slicers, time clocks, and tabulators merged to become the Computing-Tabulating-Recording Company, and Endicott operations moved into a single building operated by the Bundy brothers.

Big changes were imminent. Seeing an opportunity to more aggressively market its time clocks, tabulating machines, and food slicers, C-T-R in 1914 hired Thomas J. Watson Sr., a former top salesman for National Cash Register. Watson, in turn, immediately hired the era's best and brightest engineers, such as Fred M. Carroll, inventor of the high-speed rotary-cylinder Carroll Press, and James W. Bryce, who earned an astounding 500 patents during his career. Reflecting its role as a burgeoning "international" operation, C-T-R in 1924 changed its name to International Business Machines.

Known as the birthplace of IBM, and with roots tracing back to 1911, Endicott's history is long and colorful. Setting the early company apart was an insistence on instilling company pride through education, well-dressed employees, family outings, and a company band—such as this one outside the Endicott plant in the 1920s.

In the 1930s, IBM Endicott produced a vast number of keypunch, collating, and accounting devices for business and government. In spite of the Great Depression, Endicott continued to expand and prosper. In 1932 the first development laboratory—the North Street Lab—was built, and its distinctive clock tower remains as the site's symbol to this day. The next year, IBM dedicated its own education facility across the street. During World War II, IBM turned to producing war material at a nominal one percent profit. For its part, Endicott supplied tabulating machines and the Norden bombsight to the government. In 1944, the Automatic Sequence-Controlled Calculator, also known as the Mark I, was delivered to Harvard University for advanced military use. In 1948, the far more powerful Selective Sequence Electronic Calculator was produced and personally dedicated by Mr. Watson. Considered by many as the forerunners of modern computers, both systems were developed and assembled solely at Endicott's North Street Lab.

During the 1950s, Endicott manufactured the highly successful 1401 Processor and 1403 Printer. So reliable was the 1403, the site was producing replacement parts for units in use by customers during the late 1980s. In 1953, the world's first successful open-heart surgery took place, relying on the IBM Model II Heart-Lung machine developed and manufactured at Endicott. During the '50s period, Endicott produced the world's first commercial calculator using transistors, the IBM 608.

The 1960s brought the radically different System/360. It was the first system in the world that could use identical software across all hardware models—a fundamental principle of computing taken for granted in today's computer world. For many years, Endicott manufactured a number of System/360 models and their follow-ons.

Built in 1932, IBM Endicott's North Street Laboratory was the first facility in the entire company devoted to research and development. Currently, the facility is home to the company's Digital Video Products group, which is responsible for developing IBM digital compression and decompression chips for video and audio applications.

To meet demand from the external market and other IBM locations, Endicott produces a wide variety of high-quality products in large quantities—including about 12 million chip carriers and 1.5 million square feet of printed wiring boards a year. In this picture, an operator loads racks of chip carriers into a nickel/gold plating line for processing.

In the 1970s, the site once again demonstrated superior technical leadership by developing and manufacturing the Advanced Technology Panel. Serving as the primary packaging platform for IBM's 3090 mainframes, each panel could support modules containing 225,000 circuits. That made it the largest, most complex high-density board in the world. By the end of its product life in 1997, Endicott had produced 125,000 of the panels, enabling IBM to generate revenue of $100 billion for its mainframe line.

By the mid-'80s the site's primary missions were producing the highly popular 4381 Processor, one of the most successful mid-range computers of all time, and IBM's VM operating software.

But change for the company and the entire information technology industry was coming in the form of the most revolutionary computing device of all time—the microprocessor, which enabled the PC market to flourish. To realign itself with these fundamental changes, IBM Endicott restructured itself to the changed electronics market by bringing in new and innovative service and product missions. Other innovations took the form of environmental accomplishments. In 1994, IBM located its first-ever Asset Recovery Center at Endicott, a business venture providing state-of-the-art techniques of recovering, reusing, and reselling components and materials taken from obsolete data processing equipment. With 550,000 square feet of processing and storage space and a mile of automated conveyor systems, the center provides workload for more than 300 employees.

The site's environmental leadership takes other forms as well. In 1993, IBM Endicott completed a five-year project involving 1,000 employees to eliminate chlorofluorocarbons (CFCs) from manufacturing processes. Thanks in large part to Endicott contributions, the IBM Corporation in 1997 received the prestigious "Best-of-the-Best" award from the U.S. Environmental Protection Agency for outstanding efforts protecting the earth's stratospheric ozone layer.

Continuing its environmental legacy, in 1998 Endicott sparked the formation of the Aurora Project—a regional eco-industrial partnership comprised of business, industry, academia, and local government. Initiated to investigate reusing and recycling waste materials such as paper, glass, plastic, and industrial byproducts, the Aurora Project is seeking to manage business waste streams, minimize ecological impact, maximize business returns, sustain employment, and revitalize dilapidated or abandoned areas.

Currently the largest employer in the region, IBM Endicott takes seriously its role as a community citizen. Outside the workplace, its presence is known through activities such as Day of Caring volunteerism and charitable contributions, through which more than $1 million is donated yearly in funds and equipment to some 160 local organizations through discretionary, matching grants, and the IBM Fund for Community Service.

Through the years, virtually every division and every major IBM product has been enabled or enhanced by Endicott contributions stemming from an 80-year dedication to quality and innovation. As proof, the Endicott location earns more than 100 patents a year in hardware, software, and basic research. With only two percent of IBM's population, Endicott's 5,500 employees generate eight percent of IBM's patents.

As the original IBM location, Endicott has forged a heritage built on decades of pride in its people, products, and community. Given that historical foundation, IBM Endicott is poised to lead with products and services that excel into the next millennium. ∎

Pictured is one of these missions, the Asset Recovery Center, which annually processes some 30 million pounds of outdated or obsolete data processing equipment for its reusable and recyclable content.

Lockheed Martin Federal Systems, Owego

From the depths of the ocean to the far reaches of space, Lockheed Martin Federal Systems, Owego has played a role in national interest programs for more than 40 years. Striving for excellence with every program, from computers on the Space Shuttle to the letters delivered to your mailbox, the 3,800 Lockheed Martin employees—your friends and neighbors—have made a lasting contribution to the quality of life in the community.

Lockheed Martin Federal Systems is best known for its work in the fields of aerospace, but it is also a resource for postal systems, information technology, material handling, systems solutions, and manufacturing/industrial products.

AEROSPACE—SUCCESSFUL AND STILL GROWING

In the mid-1950s with the Cold War in full swing, the Owego facility was built to provide the bombing and navigation systems for the B-52, the pride of the U.S. Air Force. The strong engineering and scientific workforce that the facility built was a natural selection to support the space exploration program.

As digital computers began to play an increasing role in navigation and weapons delivery, 4-pi computers from the Owego facility were found on most of the nation's front-line military aircraft. Beginning with the A-6, EA-6B, A-7, and the F-111, through four generations of F-15s and continuous upgrades of the AWACS early warning aircraft, Lockheed Martin hardware has provided a war fighting advantage to our nation's military, and today that legacy continues with the F-117, U-2, B-1, C-5, and the A-10.

The technology base continued to grow and expand with a key role as prime contractor for the Lockheed Martin C-130 Combat Talon II special operations aircraft. This capability

With more than 20 years' experience on the LAMPS program, Lockheed Martin is proud to play a part in fielding the SH-60R multimission helicopter system. The centerpiece of the U.S. Navy's helicopter master plan, it is designed to meet tomorrow's wartime needs.

complements the MH-60 and MH-47 special operations helicopters, which include designed avionics from the Owego facility.

Lockheed Martin Federal Systems has been the prime contractor for integrating helicopter systems for the U.S. Navy's Light Airborne Multipurpose System since 1974. Longtime residents of the community recognize the flights of helicopters up and down the Susquehanna River as they undergo testing. Lockheed Martin is currently working with the U.S. Navy to develop a common cockpit for its entire H-60 helicopter fleet, designing systems that will be easy and economical to upgrade in the future. Those systems integration skills led to the Owego facility being selected prime contractor for the British Royal Navy's Merlin helicopter antisubmarine and antisurface warfare system.

CHANGING WITH THE TIMES

At one time, Lockheed Martin Federal Systems worked almost exclusively on projects for the military and aerospace industries, until the Department of Defense budget began to decline, and a plan was implemented to diversify and apply extensive knowledge and experience to other industries and markets. Work with postal systems and information technology systems has become, and will

The Tray Management System (TMS) is already changing the nature of material handling systems for the United States Postal Service. The TMS is a high-volume solution for moving the mail stream more productively and efficiently.

The MC-130H Combat Talon II is the behind-the-scenes "workhorse" of the special operations world. Lockheed Martin, the prime systems contractor, has pushed back the boundaries that previously limited projection of special operations forces.

continue to be, a large part of the business that Lockheed Martin does in Owego.

THE ENVELOPE, PLEASE—LOCKHEED MARTIN SPEEDS THE MAIL

Lockheed Martin is the largest supplier of technology products for the U.S. Postal Service and is involved through the entire process, from pickup to delivery. The Postal Systems business area has developed several automated readers and sorters which make mail handling faster and more accurate. One system is being installed in 250 processing centers across the country, and can read more than 300,000 addresses in an hour. Another system sorts letters into the exact sequence of the carrier's route, processing 38,000 letters per hour in 1,200 postal sites across the country. The newest device is a hand-held scanner which can record exact time of pickup and delivery.

Well-known in the material handling field, Lockheed Martin has put its knowledge to work in the postal industry. The Tray Management System helps control the movements of large mail trays in regional processing and distribution centers. Computer control helps manage a very labor-intensive process. The successful system has gone global and is now being used in Australia.

IN THE INFORMATION AGE

The incredible pace of technological change means that companies have to make changes in the way they process information. This has become an ideal opportunity for Lockheed Martin to step in with its knowledge, experience, and proven track record for working with total systems solutions. Lockheed Martin expertise is being applied to system-wide programs for global customers with household names in chemicals, telecommunications, automotive, the medical field, and those with the need to solve the "Y2K" problem.

World-class skills developed in the DoD market support Lockheed Martin Federal Systems' newest contracts in the automotive industry. Lockheed Martin will provide system maintenance, enhancements, and propose new developments for the software applications used to run General Motors' worldwide

financial systems. They also will provide operational information technology support for four processing centers, 18 parts distribution centers, and one national return center, including the information systems, operations, and maintenance of information technology hardware and software in about 30 warehousing facilities.

A GOOD NEIGHBOR—LOCKHEED MARTIN IN THE COMMUNITY

Lockheed Martin Federal Systems and its employees are dedicated to improving the quality of life in the local community through active support of and participation in programs that strengthen community services, educational excellence, and cultural enrichment.

Lockheed Martin established the Coalition for Better Schools, which has been expanded to a coalition of 12 school districts in Broome and Tioga Counties. It was established to promote and improve math and science education and to encourage students to continue study in those technical fields that will prepare them for the job market of the future.

Through the annual Charitable Contributions Campaign, Lockheed Martin employees have donated generously each year to the United Way and other community organizations. The company also donates both money and surplus equipment, like computers, to organizations in which employees are active.

INTO THE TWENTY-FIRST CENTURY—LOCKHEED MARTIN PREPARES FOR THE FUTURE

Now doing business in North America, Europe, and Australia, Lockheed Martin Federal Systems will continue to expand its expertise and services to customers around the globe. ∎

Lockheed Martin Federal Systems in Owego, New York, is a premier provider of integrated, advanced-technology system solutions for aerospace, defense, civil, and industrial customers worldwide.

Lockheed Martin Control Systems

Lockheed Martin Control Systems has been a member of the Broome County business community since 1949, when it established itself in the Southern Tier as a leader in the evolving aerospace electronics industry. Occupying a 10-acre facility formerly used by the United States Air Force to manufacture propellers, the company has grown its aerospace leadership role during the past five decades by applying new technologies and products to fit the changing face of its defense and commercial customers. More recently, the company has countered the effects of reduced defense spending through a strategy of product diversification and expansion.

Flight-critical aerospace controls are tested and their performance verified in the transport aircraft simulation laboratory. These controls are found on many of the world's high-performance airplanes.

Control Systems employs some 2,000 people at facilities in Johnson City, New York, and Fort Wayne, Indiana. An operating unit of Bethesda, Maryland-based Lockheed Martin Corporation, it began as a designer and producer of electronic systems that assisted in the control of aircraft and weapon aiming systems for bombers, fighter aircraft, and helicopters. In the 1950s, the company developed flight and weapon controls that provided automatic control for the era's faster, highly maneuverable new aircraft. These systems became the standard of excellence for high-performance aircraft control. The flight-control product line remains a core business, with flight-critical instruments installed on the world's leading aircraft platforms.

In the 1980s, Control Systems teamed with GE Aircraft Engines to provide electronic engine controls for GE jet engines.

The company maintains its relationship with GE and other engine manufacturers, providing an array of systems for both military and commercial engines.

Major product areas today include electronic systems that are critical to the flight of airplanes, electronic systems that govern the operation of aircraft engines, and aircraft computers essential to mission performance. Control Systems employees take pride in the outstanding reliability of these products on thousands of military and commercial aircraft.

In recent years, Control Systems has expanded its portfolio into areas as diverse as space flight and ground transportation. Employees in Johnson City produce sophisticated electronics that control the operation of space-launch vehicles and locomotives. And recognizing the potential for its technology to address environmental needs, the company has developed an innovative hybrid electric drive system for buses and trucks that cuts emissions, reduces fuel consumption, and improves vehicle performance. Lockheed Martin's HybriDrive™ propulsion system uses an electric motor powered by batteries that are constantly charged by an on-board generator. The technology overcomes the range limitations common to all-electric vehicles and reduces air emissions and fuel consumption by about half.

Control Systems attracts an elite workforce to the area by offering extensive opportunity for professional growth. Corporate-sponsored development programs in the fields of engineering, manufacturing, and finance teach employees the leadership and professional skills they need to become the Lockheed Martin leaders of tomorrow. All employees receive continuous training and education to maintain their competency in a progressive industry.

While its employees are dedicated to high-quality, technically

Final assembly is performed on locomotive power electronics in the Power and Drive Systems factory. Control Systems produces products for a wide variety of commercial and industrial vehicle applications.

The Johnson City plant has been the home of Control Systems since 1949, producing high-reliability electronic products for the world.

superior products, they also are committed to making the Southern Tier a better place to live. The company and its employees are generous supporters of the United Way and other local charities, including the Waterman Conservation Center, the Kopernik Space Education Center, and the Roberson Museum and Science Center. Control Systems and its employees sponsor a number of educational activities that include the Broome County Coalition for Better Schools, which promotes student interest in math and science, and technical programs at Binghamton University.

Lockheed Martin is proud of its Broome County roots. The Southern Tier has proven to be an ideal location for doing business, raising families, and making friends. ∎

An operator readies a Surface Mount Technology board for automatic component insertion. Control Systems produces most assemblies for its products, including printed circuit boards.

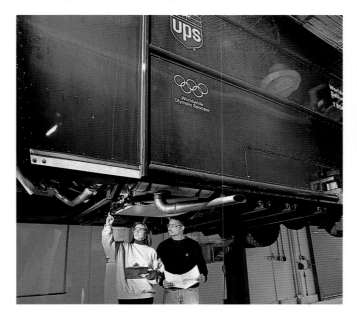

Delivery trucks and transit buses are ideal vehicles for HybriDrive™ propulsion systems. Frequent stop-and-go operation favors the economical and clean hybrid electric drive system from Lockheed Martin Control Systems.

Universal Instruments Corporation

Manufacturers in the automotive, government, consumer, telecommunications, industrial, and computer electronics industries use Universal Instruments® equipment to assemble high-quality printed circuit boards that go into the most advanced electronic products in the world.

Universal Instruments creates the machines that build the electronic circuits that go into the most advanced electronic products in the world.

Universal's assembly equipment assures a high level of productivity and quality in electronics manufacturing. Customers benefit from Universal's innovations and developments by realizing higher throughput, greater utilization, and more flexibility in their production.

From its roots as a safety pin manufacturer in 1919, Universal has grown into a multinational company with more than 1,700 employees operating in more than 30 countries. Universal Instruments is a subsidiary of Dover Corporation.

Universal's products encompass the broadest range of electronic circuit assembly solutions available from any single supplier. These solutions include equipment for surface mount, semiconductor, through hole, odd form, and light mechanical assembly.

Surface mount assembly—Universal offers GSM™ platforms specialized for material dispensing and chip, large part, and flexible-fine pitch placement, as well as high-speed chipshooters, screen printers, reflow ovens, line balancing and line optimization software, systems integration services, and board handling modules.

Advanced semiconductor assembly—Universal offers GSM platforms for flip chip placement and chip scale package production.

Through hole assembly—Radial sequencer/inserters, axial sequencers, axial sequencer/inserters, jumper wire inserters, interconnect inserters, and special machines comprise Universal's product offering for through hole technology.

Odd form and light mechanical assembly—Universal offers specialized equipment that performs connector and large odd form part placement.

Remanufactured equipment—Fully remanufactured Universal Instruments machines are available through Broome Engineering, Universal's used equipment division.

Even great assembly equipment is not enough in today's constantly changing electronics industries. Manufacturers need to know they can depend on their equipment suppliers for much more, including innovative customer support programs that help them to be successful. At Universal these include the following:

System Applications—Universal's System Applications Group integrates printed circuit board assembly equipment into complete manufacturing systems composed of all Universal or multivendor equipment. In addition, Universal's Applied Conveyor Engineering® Group designs and manufactures board handling equipment for intersystem board transport.

Project management—System Applications provides complete management of procurement, integration, installation, training, and on-line start-up projects to ensure customers get their assembly systems running smoothly.

Process consulting—Specialists in Universal's Surface Mount Technology Laboratory provide consultation and support ranging

Binghamton, New York, is home to Universal Instruments' headquarters. The company also operates eight manufacturing and administration facilities throughout Broome County.

Universal Instruments, a subsidiary of Dover Corporation, is a global leader in providing process expertise, integrated system solutions, and innovative electronic circuit assembly technology and equipment to the top manufacturers in every category of the electronics industry.

from circuit board design and solder paste selection to board and component evaluation for problem identification and process improvement.

Applications engineering—Universal's experts in assembly processes, layout engineering, control system integration, and engineering analyze customer production requirements and develop an assembly system to meet customers' specific needs.

Quality audits—Universal's Quality and Reliability Group, together with personnel from other teams within the company, provides on-site customer audits to quantify out-of-box quality, perform general manufacturing process audits, and quantify product reliability.

In addition to these support programs, Universal has a comprehensive customer service package that includes the following:

Technical support—Every Universal product is supported by technical specialists who are available for consultation by telephone to assist with machine performance questions, parts identification, and to provide other information about machine operation and servicing.

Field service—More than 200 field engineers and service representatives in offices throughout the world provide global field engineering coverage, such as machine and system installations and warranty and contract services.

Replacement parts—Universal's Worldwide Parts Sales and Distribution is a single-source supplier of high-quality replacement parts and related services for Universal Instruments electronic assembly equipment. A network of distribution centers and field support depots located around the globe bring parts closer to customers, reducing response time for critical service parts.

Training—At Product Training Centers located throughout the world, Universal offers introductory and advanced training courses on most products. The group has also developed several innovative performance support products and a "train-the-trainer" program to help manufacturers increase productivity while controlling training costs.

Continuous improvement is the foundation of Universal's Total Quality System; all Universal employees are committed to producing quality equipment and services. Since 1995, Universal's quality system has been registered to the ISO 9001 standard. This accomplishment demonstrates the company's continuing commitment to quality customer service, support, and satisfaction. ■

To help electronics manufacturers be successful, Universal has a comprehensive customer support program that includes specialized services such as the Surface Mount Technology Laboratory, which concentrates on customer-related process support.

Raytheon

In Broome County, Raytheon's roots can be traced to 1929. That was the year the first ground-based pilot training device was patented by Edwin A. Link, putting technology on a path to the skies, without ever leaving the earth. During World War II the Blue Box, as the Link Simulation Trainer was commonly known, became critical to the war effort, teaching more than half a million Allied airmen to fly by instruments.

Celestial navigation skills learned in simulation trained crews to ferry aircraft across the Atlantic at night, knowledge needed for pilots to survive under the worst conditions known to man. The local simulation industry has evolved over the years to become a worldwide leader in sophisticated high-tech systems of synthetic environments.

After nearly a quarter of a century as Link Aviation, the next five decades brought many changes in ownership. In 1954 General Precision became the parent company, and in 1968 Singer. By 1988 CAE Industries Limited came to Binghamton to blend its business talents with the growing industry. In 1995 Hughes Electronics saw the value of acquiring the veteran simulation giant. Now, the ownership has passed to Raytheon, who brings its own unique history to the incorporation.

For 75 years Raytheon has been a leader in developing defense technologies and in converting those technologies for use in commercial markets—from its early days as a maker of radio tubes, its adaptation of World War II radar technology to invent microwave cooking, and its development of the first guided missiles.

Some other impressive developments that have affected the future of the world are the First Apollo Mission simulator and the

The local simulation industry has evolved over the years to become a worldwide leader in sophisticated high-tech systems of synthetic environments.

TeleMedicine product. With the use of telecommunications, patient care in medically underserved areas is linked electronically and visually with highly trained specialists. The first air traffic control simulator was produced in 1992 to train air traffic controllers. In 1994 the B-2 aircrew trainer device was delivered to the Air Force. It was the most complex aircraft simulator ever built, able to train and duplicate two-day missions. The Mariner IV exploration of Mars was largely dependent on the Link Video Film Converter; the first nuclear power plant simulator and the mobile locomotive and train simulator, plus simulators for the Skylab and space station, are just part of the combined corporate contributions to mankind's learning process.

The complex Raytheon of today, headquartered in Lexington, Massachusetts, is an international high-technology company which operates in four business segments; Raytheon Electronics, Raytheon Systems Co., Raytheon Aircraft, and Raytheon Engineers and Construction.

Raytheon has successfully built upon its pioneering tradition to become a global technology leader. It is a top tier player in each of its core business segments. Each provides the company with the capabilities needed to build on its strength as an innovator, and to prosper in a highly competitive global economy. Raytheon is one of the largest industrial corporations in the United States, with extensive domestic and international operations serving customers in more than 80 countries throughout the world.

Operating as the Raytheon Systems Company, it is organized

Raytheon has successfully built upon its pioneering tradition to become a global technology leader.

The magic of simulation is evolving, as are the skills Raytheon employees use to continue making reality before it happens.

around segments, several of which are large enough to be among the top 500 company listings by themselves.

Producing some of the world's most sophisticated defense systems is only part of the picture. Its commercial electronics extend from outer space to the ocean depths, to the pager systems in thousands of pockets. Raytheon is developing the Main Mission Antenna transceiver system for Motorola IRIDIUM global satellite communications system, which is designed to provide wireless voice, paging, data, facsimile, and location services transmissions anywhere on earth. The process uses Raytheon's advanced gallium arsenide Monolithic Microwave Integrated Circuit technology.

Raytheon Marine is the leading supplier of marine electronics in North America, and the third largest supplier in the world. Its products guide sailors and powerboaters, and have developed tools to help fishermen using submarine sonar technology.

Raytheon Engineers and Constructors offers full-service engineering and construction capabilities to clients worldwide. And as the leading provider of business and special mission aircraft, Raytheon aircraft delivers a broad line of jet, turboprop, and piston-powered airplanes to corporate and military customers, including all areas of design, manufacture, service, logistics, and support.

The Binghamton facility is the hub for many of Raytheon's major programs, specializing in technology for the Virtual World. In the past the primary Link product has been the simulator, with

the focus on the final operation system of a training device for aircraft, space, or tank trainer.

In the future, the 450 local employees will be applying simulation in support of the development of these systems. As the field becomes more complex, the solutions will require simulation to approach true life experiences, using cutting-edge technology.

The magic of simulation is evolving, as are the skills Raytheon employees use to continue making reality before it happens. Raytheon is fully equipped to meet the needs of customers and employees into the twenty-first century and beyond. ■

For 75 years Raytheon has been a leader in developing defense technologies and in converting those technologies for use in commercial markets.

ENSCO, Inc.

ENSCO, located in Endicott, New York, provides software and systems engineering solutions to meet the business challenges faced by commercial, military, and government customers. Headquartered in Springfield, Virginia, and operating multiple national and international sites, ENSCO is a leader in critical software development and engineering technologies, including embedded real-time software, displays and graphics, critical avionics software, simulation, software test, and technical writing services. ENSCO's systems development and integration experience includes automated inspection and process control systems that are applied to a wide variety of applications, including manufacturing, material handling and distribution, warehouse management, and inventory control. ENSCO is also emerging as a leader in the development and support of commercial business systems that help many industry leaders manage their information technology needs.

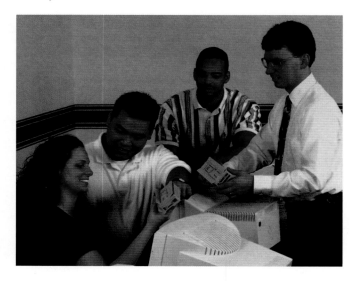

ENSCO's core business is offering its clients technical services and support in the areas of Managed Engineering Services and Software Engineering Outsourcing.

ENSCO is a leader in critical software development and engineering technologies, including embedded real-time software, displays and graphics, critical avionics software, simulation, software test, and technical writing services.

Since 1969, ENSCO has achieved industry recognition as the proven choice for exceptional technical services and products. ENSCO's core business is offering its clients technical services and support in the areas of Managed Engineering Services and Software Engineering Outsourcing. Their program management experiences range from small and midsize projects to

multimillion-dollar programs, and they have a history of building many leading corporations and government agencies. ENSCO's reputation for commitment and services has produced an impressive list of satisfied clients that include Lockheed Martin, IBM, Raytheon, and Universal Instruments.

ENSCO remains a high growth and progressive company with a total workforce of 700 employees, of which 350 people work at the Endicott facility. ENSCO provides employment stability, technical challenges, and personal growth by offering its employees impressive opportunities and rewards, including advanced career development, technical challenges, diverse work assignments, continuous investments in education and training, and a comprehensive benefits package. ENSCO is continually looking for highly skilled and talented professionals who want to share in their commitment to quality, service, innovation, and productivity. By providing its dedicated employees with a challenging and rewarding workplace and recognizing that its people are its most valuable asset, ENSCO will remain one of the preferred employers nationally as well as in Broome County.

As industries grow more complex, technological needs will call for new solutions. ENSCO anticipates these challenges with confidence and commitment. With its continual investments in resources and personnel, ENSCO will remain a leading employer. By providing proven Managed Engineering Services and Software Outsourcing Support, ENSCO will continue to produce innovative solutions that meet and exceed the high-technology challenges of today's global marketplaces. ∎

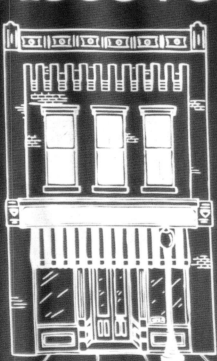

Discover

Downtown
Johnson City

c h a p t e r

BUSINESS AND FINANCE

The Broome Chamber

Broome County, nestled among the evergreen foothills of the Catskill Mountains, is known as the "valley of opportunity." Sparkling waterways and attractive communities radiate a spirit of earnest pride. Over the years there have been numerous organizations set up to improve the business sector and enhance a quality of life many already believe to be idyllic. In 1965, the Broome County Chamber of Commerce was established by uniting the individual Chambers in Johnson City, Binghamton, Endicott, Vestal, and Endwell.

The local job fairs conducted by the Recruitment Task Force of The Broome Chamber have seen a steady increase in the number of participating companies declaring that there are jobs in Broome County and plenty of good ones. Photo by Stephen J. Appel Photography.

By 1996, it became obvious that dramatic changes were needed to best serve revitalization efforts. Economic challenges inspired an initiative to unify all local community development efforts. The full affiliation of the Broome County Chamber of Commerce with the Industrial Development Agency, Economic Development Alliance, and Partnership 2000 banded local development and promotional groups into one formidable team. The Broome Chamber is now recognized as the leading economic development organization in Broome County.

Job creation and retention is the primary focus of the Industrial and Economic Development divisions of The Broome Chamber. Professional staff participate in national and international trade shows, using many award-winning marketing brochures and CD-ROMs. Other economic development priorities include expansion of the workforce and attraction of skilled labor to Broome County. As a result, a consortium of human resource executives, known as the Recruitment Task Force, takes a proactive role by conducting local job fairs, as well as promoting outside the region the high quality of life and jobs Broome County has to offer. Encouraging small businesses through innovative financial options is also a major objective, and direct loans are granted for this purpose on a regular basis.

Encouraging travelers to spend time in the area; attracting meetings, conventions, trade shows, and major events; and bringing overnight guests to Broome County are all priorities of The Broome Chamber's Convention & Visitors Bureau. Staff members produce and distribute thousands of tourism publications annually, promote the county at national trade shows, attract meeting planners to the region, and provide numerous free services to groups meeting in Broome County. The Bureau's Tourism Council facilitates an atmosphere of welcome with attraction signage, hospitality training, and visitor surveys. The Gateway Information Center, located on I-81 and operated by The Broome Chamber, assists hundreds of thousands of travelers annually, distributes New York State tourism information, and showcases current events to visitors.

A goal of The Broome Chamber's Government Relations division is advocating for legislation favorable to a progressive business climate. Serving as a liaison with local, state, and federal officials, several committees work tirelessly to reduce state business taxes and regulations, represent the county in Albany during Small Business Day, and host several legislative receptions a year. In addition, infrastructure and transportation issues are addressed with a concentration on buildings and land, utilities, and transportation.

Small businesses make up the highest percentage of Chamber membership. It is for this reason the Small Business Council was established to work on their behalf and further the development of all small businesses in Broome County. Subcommittees address issues such as continuing education, legislative concerns, networking opportunities, and recognition of exemplary performance in the small business arena with the Small Business Person and Small Business Advocate of the Year awards. Bringing the small business community together for mutual support and collaboration provides a pool of resources from which ideas and finances are drawn.

The Broome Chamber believes that the quality of life in a community depends on the quality of local leadership. Broome Leadership Institute offers people with leadership drive and commitment, the contacts, skills, and knowledge they need to assume leadership roles in community organizations or elected positions. The six-month program is designed to develop enthusiastic and well-informed leaders who are committed to making positive contributions to the community.

Providing information, securing extensive media coverage, and maintaining dialogue with local businesses and organizations is an

ongoing challenge of the Communications division of The Broome Chamber. A monthly publication provides members with vital business information; up-to-date information about Chamber functions, small business successes, and networking opportunities; economic development efforts; convention and tourism events; and legislative breaking news. In addition, recognition is given to recipients of the Distinguished Volunteer and Civic Leadership awards at the Annual Dinner. And service groups, new area executives, and individuals responsible for the positive events in our community are recognized at the annual Thanksgiving Luncheon.

Project Pride, a beautification and clean-up program sponsored by The Broome Chamber, is organized by a committee of volunteers from the business and residential community. Their mission is to improve the visual appearance of Broome County and create a more

positive impression by conducting community-wide projects such as weed and litter control, graffiti cleanup, and Adopt-A-Highway challenges.

Partnership 2000 is a private-sector fund-raising arm for economic development. Top priorities of Partnership 2000 are to encourage the purchase of goods and services locally and the continual urging of government agencies to achieve an acceptable level of efficiency. Issuing status reports on job growth and participating in regional studies to promote economic development opportunities are also part of its mission to capitalize on local economic strengths. Partnership 2000 took the initiative by forming the Southern Tier Equity Fund, whose purpose is to invest in small firms and entrepreneurs seeking to expand in Broome County.

Membership in The Broome Chamber is an investment that has prompted thousands of businesses, organizations, and individuals to join. The wide variety of assistance available to members and individuals through the Chamber include low-cost group life and health insurance, targeted marketing services, and frequent networking and social opportunities. By investing in the Chamber, businesses have the opportunity to meet potential clients, expand contacts, increase their management base, and

The Chamber's Gateway Information Center offers assistance to travelers from all over the country who are seeking information on attractions in Broome County and across New York State. Interior photo by Carriage House Photography.

become more involved in the important issues that affect our business community.

The Broome Chamber, by working in concert with the community, volunteer committees, and task forces, undertakes aggressive programs that are in the best interest of business and the community as a whole. With this unique synergy, The Broome Chamber plays a strategic role in helping shape and define Broome County's future. ■

BSB Bank & Trust

In the year 1867 BSB opened for business with an initial deposit of five cents from local industrialist and Civil War hero General Edward F. Jones. By the end of the day, total deposits came to $218.25. From that very modest beginning, BSB has grown and today, thousands of depositors and over $1.8 billion in assets later, it is the largest independent bank headquartered in New York State's Southern Tier region.

Originally incorporated as Binghamton Savings Bank, a state-chartered mutual savings bank, BSB was converted to a state-chartered stock savings bank in 1985, and in 1995 completed a charter change to that of a state-chartered commercial bank. Since 1985, it has evolved from a traditional thrift institution to a diversified financial services organization, providing a broad range of products and services to its customers. Today, BSB Bank & Trust Company is a major lender and provider of banking services to the business community and has expanded all phases of consumer lending. The bank holding company for BSB is BSB Bancorp, Inc., a Delaware corporation, which reported consolidated total assets of $1.81 billion as of September 30, 1998.

Convenience for the customer is a priority; although the headquarters remains in Binghamton, business may be conducted in many areas of Broome County, as well as Tioga, Chenango, Onondaga, and Chemung Counties and adjacent areas in New York State.

BSB has an expanding electronic delivery system that in 1998 included 35 ATMs and 12 StoreTeller locations, one located in each of the area's Giant Markets. Also recently introduced was BSB PC Home Banking, a personal interactive banking service

Since 1985, BSB has evolved from a traditional thrift institution to a diversified financial services organization, providing a broad range of products and services to its customers. Photo by Carriage House Photography.

Convenience for the customer is a priority; although the headquarters remains in Binghamton, business may be conducted in many areas of Broome County, as well as Tioga, Chenango, Onondaga, and Chemung Counties and adjacent areas in New York State.

via personal computer, a PC Bill-payer service, and Telephone-Teller. By the introduction of these new electronic services and the enhancement of the existing electronic delivery systems, customers have 24-hour service from many off-site locations. The future of electronic banking is here today at BSB.

BSB is a leader in residential mortgage originations in Broome County. It takes very seriously its responsibility to ensure that all qualified individuals have access to home ownership through mortgage financing. As such, the company participates in several programs which provide financing equally to all racial, ethnic, and income groups. They are committed to meeting the housing financing needs of all segments of the population. The array of loan products presently available through the BSB branch system and through third-party originators is without equal in the marketplace. In addition, these products are delivered in an efficient and "customer friendly" manner, consistent with a strong commitment to personal service and responsiveness to consumer needs.

BSB is the leading business lender in Broome County. Critical to the success of the BSB commercial lending program is the

BSB is the leading business lender in Broome County. Photo by Carriage House Photography.

excellent staff of commercial lenders who have built strong banking relationships with the customers they serve. The loyalty that has resulted from the staff's commitment to superior service is highly beneficial to the bank and the whole community. BSB believes its capacity to provide financing for virtually all the needs of small- and medium-sized businesses, working capital, equipment, real estate, etc. is a cornerstone of success for the future.

As part of BSB's commitment to serving an informed community, Internet access is available at www.bsbbank.com. Extensive information on the bank's financial performance, features, products, services, and interactive loan and financial services information may be easily reviewed and downloaded for future reference.

In 1996 BSB Financial Services was formed to provide an expanded selection of financial products to customers. This bank subsidiary concentrates on providing comprehensive, personal financial planning and a broad array of investment and insurance products. Also provided are brokerage and insurance services, financial planning, mutual funds, individual stocks, and bonds, as well as annuity and insurance products through INVEST Financial Corporation.

Trust services have become an important facet of the BSB business. An increasing number of individuals are naming BSB Bank & Trust as executor or trustee of their wills. This department has the experience, the resources, and the expertise to take care of virtually every detail of important matters such as custodian agreements, Trustee of Retirement Plans, and Trustee under Agreement/Living Trusts.

Expanding from a leadership position in BSB's traditional home market, it recently established a new business banking office in downtown Syracuse. It is a fully staffed branch that serves the needs of a growing customer base in Onondaga County. The new office provides geographic diversification of the company's loan

mix and is bringing the kind of value-added relationship banking to this market that has made them so successful elsewhere.

Most of all, BSB is thoroughly community oriented, supporting numerous charities and art and cultural organizations. This volunteer service goes beyond a corporate dollar commitment. It is a people investment, a personal employee commitment to the needs of others. BSB officers and staff serve on boards of directors, volunteer where needed, and participate in fund-raising walks and runs to give their neighbors a chance at a better life. Caring about people has been part of BSB's belief since 1867, and the corporation continues to give credit for its success to the depositors, the people who had the vision and the thrift and the confidence to help build a stable future.

Customers can visit one of the numerous offices in person, do business with StoreTeller and MachineTeller banking partners, or reach them by phone, fax, or PC. They are available, on some basis, 24 hours a day, seven days a week. And while an increasing number of customers want to interact with them via Touch-Tone™ phone or computer modem, the most popular methods are still voice-to-voice and face-to-face. It is this type of contact that develops and maintains the most enduring banking relationships. Meeting the customers' financial needs with the highest standards of integrity and ethical behavior is a way of doing business they have been practicing for 132 years. ■

Today, BSB Bank & Trust Company is a major lender and provider of banking services to the business community and has expanded all phases of consumer lending. Photo by Carriage House Photography.

Security Mutual Life Insurance Company of New York

In 1886, Charles Turner had an idea that gave birth to Security Mutual. He believed in providing a high-quality product at a competitive price, and he convinced many Binghamton businessmen to join him in founding a new insurance company. More than 110 years later, Security Mutual is a recognized leader in providing innovative insurance products and services, and in supporting the local community.

Since 1997, the second week in September has been designated "Security Mutual Week" in downtown Binghamton. During that week the company celebrates its field, employee, and community partnerships, and the City of Binghamton proudly displays flags bearing Security Mutual's arch.

In its second century of service, Security Mutual's mission is based on the same values upon which Charles Turner founded the company—to provide sound, equitable, and competitive financial protection against financial hazards resulting from premature death or disability.

Unlike a stock company, Security Mutual was established as a mutual life association so that policyowners, not private investors, would share its profits. Today, the company is still a mutual company, owned by and operated for the benefit of its policyowners. A New York-domiciled company, Security Mutual operates under the regulation of the New York State Insurance Department, among the strongest and most respected insurance departments in the country.

A RICH HISTORY

Security Mutual officially opened its doors for business on January 3, 1887. On that day, it sold its first policy: a one-year renewable term policy with a death benefit of $1,000. The entire company filled two small offices in the old MacNamara Building at 86 Court Street.

Security Mutual immediately established itself as an innovator in the insurance industry. In 1889 it became the first company in the nation to offer what, at the time, was a revolutionary concept: disability benefits. In 1900, during the height of prohibition, the company established the "Total Abstinence League," offering members a preferred class policy if they agreed not to use, manufacture, or sell intoxicating liquors of any form. This offering was enormously popular and once again demonstrated the value of product innovation in a competitive industry.

THE HISTORIC SECURITY MUTUAL BUILDING

Security Mutual continued to prosper, and in 1904 began construction of a 10-story home office building at the corner of Court and Exchange Streets. The arched stone entranceway was designed after the arched stone bridge depicted in the company's original logo, and symbolizes safety and strength.

Designed in the French Renaissance style, the Security Mutual Building is a steel frame "skyscraper" with a brick and masonry facade. Inside, the building reflects the splendor and craftsmanship of a bygone era. The arched entranceway leads to a two-story lobby that is 38 feet tall and finished in Pavonezza and Carrara marble. Twin marble staircases curve gracefully to the building's second floor, and the carved marble head of a dog stands guard over the entranceway.

On the eighth floor, the walls are paneled in walnut, and several of the office floors are intricately patterned in a variety of hardwoods. Several of the offices, including the boardroom, have fireplaces, where fires once burned for warmth during the winter months. The doorknobs leading to the executive offices were specially cast, with the company emblem reproduced in exquisite detail in gleaming brass.

Throughout the years, Security Mutual has shared its home office with a number of business tenants, including a bank, a music company, a restaurant, a barbershop, and a steam bath. In fact, the Preservation Society of the Southern Tier notes that during the Depression, the first floor housed a restaurant and lounge that featured a number of famous performers, including Lionel Hampton, Eddie Heywood, Don Hickey, and a young Liberace.

Security Mutual continued to grow, and in 1981 the company completed an addition to the back of the building, providing 95,000 square feet of new office space. The addition is built around a dramatic two-story, plant-filled atrium capped by three skylights.

Security Mutual's Home Office is now considered a landmark building in downtown Binghamton, where it continues to stand as a symbol of stability and financial protection.

A STRONG COMPANY, A BRIGHT FUTURE

To meet its customers' business and personal needs, the company offers a complete line of life insurance products and financial services, including annuities, financial- and retirement-planning services, and a variety of individual and group life insurance policies.

From $15,000 in assets its first year in existence, Security Mutual has grown to more than $1.4 billion in assets, with more than $21.4 billion of life insurance in force. The company is staffed by more than 300 employees, and its products are distributed by over 5,500 independent agents throughout the United States and U.S. Virgin Islands.

For the past consecutive 106 years, Security Mutual has paid dividends to its policyowners, with 74 percent of the company's 1998 earnings going to policyowners in the form of dividend payments. The company continues to achieve superior results in its investment portfolio without sacrificing quality or accepting the risk of extreme positions. More than 99.6 percent of the company's bond portfolio is within investment-grade categories as defined by the National Association of Insurance Commissioners. In fact, Security Mutual is recognized by leading insurance analysts for its sound investment policies and performance: the company is rated "A" by A. M. Best, "A+" by Duff and Phelps, and "A+" by Standard & Poor's.

In 1998 Security Mutual became one of only 155 companies nationwide to achieve membership in the Insurance Marketplace Standards Association (IMSA). This achievement demonstrates the company's long-standing commitment to serve its customers in accordance with high standards of honesty and fairness.

While accomplishing these outstanding results, Security Mutual has also concentrated on strategically positioning itself to grow and prosper well beyond the turn of this century. The company continually monitors marketplace developments, developing new products and refining existing products to fill its clients'

From its landmark Home Office building in downtown Binghamton, Security Mutual has provided financial protection for over 100 years. The company is staffed by 330 home office employees, and its products are distributed by over 5,500 independent agents throughout the United States and U.S. Virgin Islands.

financial-planning needs. Security Mutual has also made significant investments in technology to ensure that in the next millennium, the necessary tools and infrastructure are in place so employees can continue providing the high level of service and support required by the company's customers.

COMMITMENT TO THE COMMUNITY

Not only is Security Mutual a major employer in downtown Binghamton, but the company has also created new downtown office space through its recent restoration of the 104-year-old building at 105-107 Court Street.

Security Mutual employees consider themselves partners in the success of Broome County. These dedicated individuals donate both time and money to a wide variety of charitable events and organizations, including the United Way, school mentoring programs, hospitals, health foundations, and youth sports programs. In addition, Security Mutual is a corporate sponsor of the Binghamton Summer Music Festival, as well as of Binghamton's First Night celebration, and SML President and CEO Bruce Boyea is serving as chairman of the Year 2000 Empire State Games, which will be held in Broome County.

Security Mutual . . . Your Partner for Life. ■

The Security Mutual Building reflects the splendor and craftsmanship of a bygone era. The arched entranceway leads to a two-story lobby finished in Pavonezza and Carrara marble, with twin marble staircases leading to the building's second floor.

Chase Manhattan Bank

The Chase Manhattan Bank has been part of Southern Tier communities for nearly 150 years. In 1852 the City National Bank was established in downtown Binghamton, and in 1863 The First National Bank opened its doors for business. By 1955 it became obvious that a merger of these two historic institutions would provide the area with a major banking presence. Since that time, every decade has been marked by corporate growth through significant combinations of financial concerns. With 14 local branches and 130 employees, Chase's commitment to the Southern Tier is seen in every facet of Broome and surrounding counties.

Chase's main office is located on the bank of the beautiful Chenango River. Designed for compatibility with the surroundings and customer convenience, the building is both striking and graceful. An outstanding feature of the main lobby is a 49-foot-long, 6-foot-high handwoven tapestry showing a turn-of-the-century view of the Chenango River at sunset. The magnificent work of art sets the tone for the financial institution, an expression of expanding a solid heritage into the high-tech future.

However, the influence and scope of Chase extends far beyond these borders. The corporation is a money center bank, dealing in worldwide finance. It is one of the largest banks in the world, providing "the cutting edge" of all banking products to the Southern Tier businesses and individuals.

(left to right) Dale Lutz serves as Chase Manhattan's Binghamton regional commercial banking executive, and Joan Clow is the Binghamton regional retail banking executive. All Chase Manhattan photos by Carriage House Photography.

The banking facility is divided into three powerful business platforms: Global Banking, National Consumer Services, and Chase Technology Solutions.

The Global Banking unit is among the industry's largest and most profitable global banking franchises. The Global Banking unit has earned a broad and diverse client base, a leadership position across a full spectrum of products and geographies, and a track record of executing the complex "one-stop," multifaceted transactions that characterize wholesale financing today. This platform enables Chase to bring together the best of commercial and investment banking.

The Chase Global presence is an integrated network with a client base encompassing more than 5,000 major corporations and institutions in 180 countries. Chase ranks first by a large margin in primary banking relationships and is a lead banker to the major financial sponsors, issuers, and investors of the world. Money markets the world over regard Chase with trust. The impressive global trading powerhouse is guided by, and brought to, Broome County by "hometown" people who combine an understanding of the needs of local business customers with the capabilities of this powerful franchise.

Chase's National Consumer Services franchise has more than 30 million customers coast to coast. Created by integrating Chase's regional and nationwide businesses into a single platform, they combine market leadership across a broad range of products, including nationwide companies for credit card, mortgage banking, and auto finance. In automobile financing, Chase is a leading

By creating solutions for customers, opportunities for employees, and superior returns for shareholders, Chase is achieving the goal of being a banking leader with integrity.

bank lender, used by more than 7,000 car dealerships across the country. In mortgage banking, prospective home buyers may access Chase through an Internet page that is recognized as one of the best in the industry. Products ranging from mutual funds and insurance to smart cards and banking by computer maximize Chase's recognition for quality services, making the banking firm an asset to every American household. Its focus is on building and extending relationships with consumers, using a wide range of delivery channels and the marketing intelligence made possible by new applications of technology.

The Technology Solutions area is a newly aligned transaction processing platform bringing together Chase's high-return, market-leading global services business—custody, cash management, and trust services—with the corporation's information technology division. Leading edge information and transaction processing capabilities and a wide range of electronic commerce initiatives make banking associations both convenient and powerful. Combining these information-intensive businesses under unified management enables Chase to capitalize on its scale, efficiency, and investment capabilities.

The corporate vision captures the essence of what business should be—an entity guided by integrity and respect for both clients and employees, with a sense of social responsibility for the needs of the community. Continual investment in the arts, culture, city infrastructure revitalization, and educational grants highlights Chase's active support in organizations and programs designed to optimize a favorable impact on living standards. Offering programs for the handicapped, housing opportunities, credit counseling services, minority enterprises, and elderly concerns are just a few of the bank's investments in humanity. Hundreds of thousands of dollars are donated, but equally important are the personal hours contributed by employees in volunteerism—neighbors serving as examples and partners in the future. Chase's corporate initiatives in philanthropic endeavors are geared to

Chase is a complete financial resource and ally for enhancing the well-being of our communities, both local and global.

improving the quality of life through ongoing participation. Charitable and technical support to nonprofit organizations is offered throughout the United States and overseas.

In Broome County, Chase has a Trust tradition dating back to its predecessors and continuing today as the largest Trust Department in the area. The Global Trust and Investment resources available help to provide state-of-the-art solutions to the needs of many local individuals and institutions.

The Chase approach to success is the corporate team dedication to providing quality, initiative, and professionalism—fundamental values rooted in a commitment to integrity in all aspects of business. Fairness and opportunity for all employees have produced an outstanding staff of the highest quality people at all levels dedicated to offering the client the best service possible. The management targets are all driven by the goal of successful customer relationships. Financial services are specifically tailored to contribute to the prosperity of individuals and businesses. By creating solutions for customers, opportunities for employees, and superior returns for shareholders, Chase is achieving the goal of being a banking leader with integrity.

The brand recognition of The Chase Manhattan Corporation is worldwide, and the future promises an even more comprehensive array of product options through the use of technology and the ever-expanding nonbranch channels in service delivery. The goal is always to make life easier for individuals and businesses, producing a new standard in quality, convenience, and choice, anywhere, at any time, and in any form that suits a client's needs. Chase is a complete financial resource and ally for enhancing the well-being of our communities, both local and global. ■

The Chase approach to success is the corporate team dedication to providing quality, initiative, and professionalism—fundamental values rooted in a commitment to integrity in all aspects of business.

Visions Federal Credit Union

Offering a wide variety of quality financial products and services, Visions Federal Credit Union has been serving the financial needs of its members since 1965, when the IBM Owego Federal Credit Union was established for the purpose of providing low-cost financial services to IBM employees and their families.

The following year, IBM employees in Endicott chartered a second credit union much the same way as their Owego counterparts.

In 1981 the two credit unions were merged and operated as the IBM Endicott\Owego Employees Federal Credit Union until 1994. At that time, recognizing the need to more accurately reflect their expanding member base, the name was changed to Visions Federal Credit Union.

Today, Visions Federal Credit Union is one of the most progressive and financially sound credit unions in the country,

Automated services provide 24-hour member service. Pictured is the ITC office in Endicott. Photo by Carriage House Photography.

with over 200 employees serving over 80,000 members nationwide.

Credit Union members are also owners. That's the Credit Union difference. As a member/owner, members have an important role in determining the direction their credit union should take to best meet their needs. Because credit unions are nonprofit cooperatives, members receive better rates, lower fees, and maximum convenience.

To meet the ever-growing needs of its membership, Visions Credit Union has developed one of the most sophisticated electronic delivery systems available in the financial services industry.

An extensive network of ATMs, Audio Response, and Internet services are available to members 24 hours a day, seven days a week.

With branch/ATM locations throughout the Triple Cities and the Southern Tier, the Credit Union is able to conveniently serve the financial needs of over 150 selected employer groups.

In addition to offering traditional loan and savings products, the credit union provides members with added services including investments/financial planning; home, auto, and life insurance; tax preparation; and discount brokerage.

Although it consistently receives superior financial ratings, Visions does not measure its success on financial performance alone. It is committed to the Credit Union philosophy of "People Helping People" and to being an active, involved part of the communities it serves.

With a balance of outstanding service and quality financial products, Visions Federal Credit Union is prepared to meet the challenges of the twenty-first century. ■

Visions Federal Credit Union serves members with 15 offices throughout the Southern Tier. Shown here is the Oakdale Mall office in Johnson City. Photo by Carriage House Photography.

Tri-Town Insurance

One of the greatest human needs is security—protection from the loss of life and goods. We have a need to assure a future for our progeny—to provide a comfort zone in a world of change and challenges. And derived from the word "assure," comes insurance.

Tri-Town Insurance has been in the business of providing security for its clients since 1925. Headquartered in a building constructed in 1890, located on the historic River Row in Owego, New York, with offices in the surrounding towns, Tri-Town is an independent insurance agent and brokerage firm representing all the major "A"-rated insurance companies in the United States.

In 1977 A. Thomas Poulton took the helm, and the intervening years have seen growth and prosperity, spiraling in a 40-mile radius encompassing Owego. Since 1980 Tri-Town has led the way in computerization, which translates into efficient and accurate claim handling when its insureds need it most. With clients in Broome, Chenango, Cortland, Delaware, and Tioga Counties, service is extremely important to the success and handling of clients' needs. Realizing the importance of claims and service to its clientele early in the automation era, all of Tri-Town's locations are connected by a sophisticated computer system. This enables a shared database so clients may obtain assistance at any location, no matter which office the policies were purchased.

Building on heritage, Tri-Town takes great pride in being an integral part of the communities it serves, in knowing the people and businesses on a personal level. Committed relationships with clients is the primary goal in providing the most appropriate coverage and service. Any type of insurance from commercial, municipal, nonprofit organizations, personal, and benefit plans, including long-term care, are available. Tri-Town's interest is to provide all the insurance and money services that an individual, family, or business may need forever.

Time is willingly given by professional, licensed agents and brokers who offer options and guidance in a professional manner. In-depth analysis of personal or corporate requirements is a lengthy process, but is necessary to devise the best program of insurance for the client. For an added convenience, various payroll deduction programs are available.

Trust and confidence are earned by the staff every day. Ongoing education is required of associates to keep up-to-date on the changing insurance, financial, and benefits industry. This valuable information is passed on to clients so that educated choices in risk assumption can be accomplished. Many types of insurance questions are continually addressed by people who are serious about client satisfaction.

As an independent agency, Tri-Town Insurance is able to take advantage of the competitive rates among the best insurance providers in the nation, obtaining the most economical premiums for clients. The unique characteristics of the Tri-Town Agency are exemplified by the company vision; it plans to be in the insurance business providing long-term service and solutions for people and commerce forever—not just for the short term—offering security and care for the whole life. So when someone is confronted by the "Slings and arrows of outrageous fortune," Tri-Town will be there as experts and friends, a partner in life. The corporate slogan "We're Lookin' Out For You!" is truly what each of Tri-Town's longtime educated staff does day in and day out. ■

Tri-Town Insurance is proud to be a part of Broome County. Photo by Van Zandbergen Photography.

c h a p t e r

PROFESSIONS

Coughlin & Gerhart, LLP

Laws are created to govern the affairs of mankind. Laws strengthen the bonds of justice so individuals may enjoy "life, liberty, and the pursuit of happiness," within acceptable perimeters. But laws are only as just as those who represent the legal system. Broome County has been fortunate to have the firm of Coughlin & Gerhart, LLP acting as law officers since the 1890s. Adding to their long-standing reputation for conscientious and superior service, the firm has recently merged with another century-old organization—Twining, Nemia & Steflik, who have been serving regional and national clients since 1892. The history of both firms is entwined in the annals of Broome County, as integral partners in the development of the area.

A major field of practice includes corporate and business law. It encompasses many of the vital problems which arise in the business world.

As a full-service law firm with 30 active lawyers, Coughlin & Gerhart is expanding the practice in many directions. Being a regional concern, the main office remains in downtown Binghamton, but branch offices have been opened in numerous cities in the Southern Tier of New York and the Northern Tier of Pennsylvania. In recent years the arena of labor law has increased significantly because of the numerous federal and state statutes dealing with employers and their employees. By combining strengths with Twining, Nemia & Steflik, expertise has been added in the employment and labor law and litigation practice. They now have a highly reputable and experienced group of four attorneys devoting full time to complicated labor relations and employment matters.

Another major field of practice includes corporate and business law. It encompasses many of the vital problems which arise in the business world. It is responsible for dealing with lenders,

corporations, partnerships, limited liability companies, and commercial transactions in general. This group also covers municipal and public sector law clients, banks, and financial institutions.

The firm's real estate lawyers have considerable experience in commercial mortgage lending, construction lending, subdivision development, and residential mortgages, plus preparation and review of industrial development revenue bonds. Complicated zoning matters, title insurance, land use, and environmental problems are all carefully handled. They are also authorized to act on behalf of the Federal Housing Administration and many of New York State's largest title insurance companies.

In the litigation group, the firm's general civil practice is conducted throughout the local, state, and federal courts at both the trial and appellate levels. Municipalities, corporations, and individual plaintiffs and defendants in commercial, products liability, and personal injury action are all represented. Because of the litigation department's commendable dedication, countless products, workplaces, and business facilities are safer for the public. They are extremely proud of their contribution to the well-being of each client.

Trusts, estates, and taxation are the specialty of the last group of attorneys. Expert handling of estate planning, wills, trusts, pension and profit sharing matters, tax advice, probate and administration of estates, as well as estate litigation, are just part of the responsibilities they deal with on a regular basis. Asset protection, elder law and health care matters, divorce, separation, adoption, and family court cases receive compassionate, competent counsel.

Each lawyer in the practice realizes the importance of building a long-term relationship with clients, based on friendly, mutual understanding. They also believe every member should do their

The firm's real estate lawyers have considerable experience in commercial mortgage lending, construction lending, subdivision development, and residential mortgages, plus preparation and review of industrial development revenue bonds.

The firm has a highly reputable and experienced group of four attorneys devoting full time to complicated labor relations and employment matters.

part for country and community. Several of the attorneys have been listed in the "Who's Who in Law," recognized for excellence in the legal profession.

Firm attorneys have served in the military in every conflict since World War I, and have served the United States in the political arena and in judgeships. Coughlin & Gerhart, LLP has produced two presidents of the New York Bar Association, one editor in chief of the *New York State Bar Journal,* several presidents of the Broome County Bar Association, and a minority and majority leader of the New York State Assembly. Many are still giving time on the boards of various local charities, universities, and the Broome County Chamber of Commerce. Numerous articles and other legal writings have been produced by staff attorneys for publication. One notable member has been responsible for writing legal biographies and collections of legal articles and quotations, all highly praised by both the public and the legal profession. Pro bono publico and legal aid assistance are part of the professional profile, and leadership qualities are encouraged in business and private life as a further expression of dedication to the area.

Technologically, the firm is at the leading edge of worldwide legal access. Using the most up-to-date systems and highly trained staff for support, clients can be assured of receiving the highest quality legal counsel delivered in a cost-efficient and timely manner. Built on a long history of exemplary service, it is a

forward-looking firm using the very latest technologies offered by business and industry to expedite work for clients. In order to maintain the highest standards, great emphasis is placed on continuing education. As an expression of commitment, programs and courses are offered at the expense of the firm.

The ideals of the founders of integrity and quality advocacy are maintained by the skilled attorneys of today who carry on the tradition of excellence. They offer representation to corporations and individual clients in all areas of legal need, giving sound, responsive counsel. Diversity, extensive experience, and honor are the hallmarks for Coughlin & Gerhart, LLP, who may not be the largest firm in number of attorneys, but is second to none in fundamental decency and trust in the practice of law. ∎

In the litigation group, the firm's general civil practice is conducted throughout the local, state, and federal courts at both the trial and appellate levels.

McFarland-Johnson, Inc.

A touch of historic class, state-of-the-art computer/CADD equipment, and some of the best trained and most dedicated people in the business equal McFarland-Johnson, Inc. Since 1946, the multidiscipline consulting firm has been providing innovative and economical solutions to engineering, planning, and environmental service needs. It is the largest consulting engineering firm in New York's Southern Tier, as well as in Broome County.

The firm has built its organization and reputation on the ideals of sound principles and superiority in engineering design. Utilizing high-tech, state-of-the-art computer/CADD design techniques in engineering applications challenges the staff to exceed client expectations. They are committed to providing quality work in all major areas of planning, surveying, engineering, and construction administration for civil, environmental, mechanical, electrical, and structural projects.

The experienced staff can offer solutions for every challenge. A team can be assembled with in-house professionals with specialized skills to manage all phases of developing a facility. The multidisciplinary approach provides clients with the economy and convenience of using a single consulting firm, no matter how complex a project's specifications. Meeting aggressive schedules for emergency response and fast-track requirements is a priority. The

company specializes in taking a project from concept to completion, on schedule and within budget. Complete on-site expertise is available from any of their six northeast locations: Woodbury, New Jersey; Concord, New Hampshire; Burlington, Vermont; Norwich, Conneticut; New Milford, Pennsylvania; and from its headquarters office in Broome County, New York.

The Clinton Street Family Care Center—United Health Services in Binghamton is a proud McFarland-Johnson client.

McFarland-Johnson performed the mechanical and electrical engineering for WBNG, Channel 12 Studio in Johnson City, New York.

McFarland-Johnson has designed facilities and transportation projects for various industrial and commercial owners, federal agencies, airports, and state and municipal governments, as well as buildings for schools, hospitals, and other institutions. The use of in-house drafting and design personnel using the most advanced CADD systems for engineering design applications and an intensive Quality Assurance Program have made it possible to give personal attention and complete satisfaction to each client.

As a 100-percent Employee Stock Ownership Plan (ESOP) company, pride of ownership gives each member of the staff an investment in providing excellent service, and in maintaining a work environment which fosters professional and personal development through challenging opportunities and employee involvement.

Using knowledge gained from over 50 years in the industry, McFarland-Johnson has much more than just the basic qualifications to meet engineering needs. The presence of numerous retired state and local government and agency officials on their staff makes them particularly well suited to expedite a client's project through the various permit phases/processes, as well as providing insight and assistance in obtaining government grants, if desired. The firm is dedicated to continuing its tradition of establishing long-term relationships with clients through ethical, responsive, and quality solutions. McFarland-Johnson aggressively pursues planned growth, new technologies, and visions for the future as "Your Partner in Progress." ■

The Haworth Press, Inc.

Since 1978 The Haworth Press has been filling the niches and needs of the printed word industry. Honoring two of Britain's literary legends, the name was taken from the English township which was the home of the famous Brontë sisters. From modest beginnings with only a post office box for a home base, to its current large facilities in Binghamton and Kirkwood, New York, and Hazleton, Pennsylvania, The Haworth Press, Inc. has become a major player in scholarly publishing. Currently, the firm publishes over 170 journals and 80 new books per year.

Quality and diversity are the guidelines for the 2,000 books and hundreds of journals The Haworth Press publishes. As premier publisher in a wide range of academic and popular subjects, it is often the only outlet for professionals who need to be represented in the marketplace. During its first 20 years the firm identified niche areas in major disciplines and continues to dominate the industry in areas determined to be "hot topics." Haworth has clustered major publication programs under subsidiary divisions, according to their editorial and market identities. Everything from social work, pharmaceuticals, herbal medicine, business, pastoral care, travel and hospitality, alternative lifestyles, and agriculture are included in the vast array of textbooks, guidebooks, reference books, and journals published by The Haworth Press. Each editor is a highly regarded and distinguished specialist in their respective field.

A unique feature of The Haworth Press is that it is completely self-contained. It is one of the few publishing houses that actually produces all of its own books and journals utilizing an entirely

A unique feature of The Haworth Press is that it is completely self-contained. It is one of the few publishing houses that actually produces all of its own books and journals utilizing an entirely in-house production system.

The Haworth Press, Inc. has become a major player in scholarly publishing. Currently, the firm publishes over 170 journals and 80 new books per year.

in-house production system. All work is produced on high-speed digital laser printers. The use of laser technology means that on-demand printing is cost-effective, making print runs of any size feasible. The complete digital generation guarantees no book will ever be out of print. Combining state-of-the-art technology with vintage methods, they produce their own hardcovers. Haworth was the first business in the United States, and the ninth in the world, to use a new film laminating process combining paper and plastic to create breathable soft covers for books that will hold their shape. Two four-color printers give the company the capacity to produce book and journal covers in spectacular colors.

By aggressively modernizing production facilities, journal information is available on-line through the Internet and the World Wide Web, http://haworthpressinc.com. A sampling of nearly 200 journals and a catalog of publications featuring descriptive information allows for easy perusal and purchasing. Electronic delivery is expanding services available to consumers in this growing medium.

As technology changes, so will Haworth's approach to the development of its products, production methods, and marketing. Knowing that success is built on the strength of its staff, maintaining a commitment to employees and the community remains a priority. These ideals will carry this publishing house into the new millennium and beyond. ■

Hinman, Howard & Kattell, LLP

For nearly a century, Hinman, Howard & Kattell, LLP has been building a tradition of public service. In 1902 the firm was founded by three young attorneys, New York State Senator Harvey D. Hinman, Archibald Howard, and Thomas B. Kattell. By January 1999 the firm reached a level of 70 lawyers and more than 80 support staff personnel, occupying four floors in downtown Binghamton in the historic Security Mutual Life Insurance Building. Additional branch offices have been opened in Oneonta, Norwich, and New York City, New York. It is currently the largest law firm in the Southern Tier region of New York State. Personnel often establish lifelong careers with the firm, providing stability and continuity of representation.

James W. Orband is managing partner of Hinman, Howard & Kattell, LLP.

Decades of confidence in the Hinman firm have been exhibited by nationally notable individuals such as Charles Evans Hughes, former Governor of New York State and later Chief Justice of the United States, who chose Senator Hinman as a confidant. Senator Hinman's son, George L. Hinman, was appointed a member of the New York State Board of Regents and became a personal advisor to Governor of New York State and Vice President of the United States Nelson A. Rockefeller.

Many of the firm's attorneys have attained distinguished public careers, notably Warren M. Anderson, State of New York Minority Leader of the State Assembly. Members of the Board of Trustees of the State University of New York, and a Surrogate's Court judge have also been among the firm's personnel.

Caring for the community is a way of life for the firm's attorneys. Many are leaders in activities such as the Broome County Chamber of Commerce, the United Way of Broome County, the state and local Bar Associations and their discipline and ethics committees, and a host of other nonprofit foundations, arts, and human service organizations. Society continues to benefit from this gift of time.

For nearly a century, leading businesses, as well as individual clients from around the nation, have chosen counsel from Hinman, Howard & Kattell. The first priority of the firm is producing a high quality of legal service in a timely manner. All work is tailored to the need, whether in litigation, negotiation, or client counseling, to the practical demands of each situation and the specific needs of the companies and individuals with whom they work. A broad, comprehensive range of legal concentrations that cover every spectrum of human need is offered. All services are provided by attorneys who have motivation and common sense, and who have excelled in academic achievement.

The area's most complete in-house law library is complemented by computerized research facilities for instant access to United States and worldwide law data. As the firm heads into its second century, it plans to expand and amplify technology for keeping pace with ever-changing laws.

Hinman, Howard & Kattell has the experience, resources, and skill to provide effective legal advice and representation in transactions and litigation, with courtesy and high ethical standards. ■

For nearly a century, leading businesses, as well as individual clients from around the nation, have chosen counsel from Hinman, Howard & Kattell. James Orband proudly poses with the portrait of George L. Hinman, a member of the New York State Board of Regents and personal advisor to Nelson A. Rockefeller.

Fred Riger Advertising Agency

"Your idea will never fly!" That's what people told Fred Riger nearly 50 years ago, when they heard about his plan to leave a good public relations job in New York City and return to his hometown to open an advertising agency of his own. It wasn't the best advice to give to a battle-tested former bomber pilot whose resolve had been hardened while flying dozens of combat missions in World War II. He wanted to establish a first-rate advertising agency in the Southern Tier region of upstate New York, and that's what he set out to do.

Starting with a skeleton staff, a few local clients, and an indomitable spirit, Fred accepted the challenge and began building the impossible dream—the best and largest advertising agency in south central New York State and northeastern Pennsylvania.

From the beginning, Fred realized that sales drive the economy. He was often heard to say "nothing happens until somebody sells something," and the way to sales success is paved with good, solid advertising. These principles, along with honesty, integrity, and a strong work ethic, served the agency well, as did Fred's belief that a diversified client roster benefited both agency and client. To prove his point, he enjoyed demonstrating to clients how lessons learned while supporting McDonald's efforts to sell more hamburgers in the Southern Tier could also help a high-tech manufacturing company increase its market share overseas.

Fred also believed strongly in meaningful, long-term client relationships. That belief has resulted in associations with clients of 40 years and more. It also has provided Riger people with plenty of opportunities to get involved with their client counterparts in virtually every phase of the marketing communications process—and beyond. It has meant pitching in during major sales events,

manning trade show exhibits, even attending "patty flipping" classes, and on occasion, assisting busy McDonald's store crews in the heat of lunch-hour battle. No matter if grilling one's tie along with the burger was not part of the standard procedure.

Riger people are proud of their agency's legacy of running a diversified, results-oriented advertising agency, doing its homework, and recognizing that the best creative solutions often come from looking at things a little bit differently. The agency's first-class writers, designers, and producers are willing to take a chance, when necessary, to get the best results for their clients. After all, they know that achieving the desired results is the real measure of success.

Peter Cronk and Jon Davis, who both benefited from Fred Riger's mentoring early in their careers, have been the agency's managing partners since his retirement in 1984. Together with fellow partners Mark Bandurchin and Steve Johnson, they have expanded the geographical reach of the agency, broadened its menu of services, and generally enhanced the "Riger" brand. As for the future, people at Riger are enthusiastic about the new directions and opportunities technology and globalization are bringing about. As for Fred's maxim—"Nothing happens until somebody sells something"—it's just as true today as ever before. And the Riger dream is in full flight. ■

Riger people are proud of their agency's legacy of running a diversified, results-oriented advertising agency, doing its homework, and recognizing that the best creative solutions often come from looking at things a little bit differently.

Levene, Gouldin & Thompson, LLP

The stately brick office building on Plaza Drive which is the home of Levene, Gouldin & Thompson, LLP gives an aura of strength and stability—an image consistent with the law firm's long-standing reputation for sound advice and successful advocacy. For more than 70 years, Levene, Gouldin & Thompson has been providing individuals and businesses in the Southern Tier of New York with a wide range of personal and corporate legal services. The ability to offer prompt, practical, result-oriented counsel has made the firm one of the largest and most respected law offices in the state of New York. With more than 40 attorneys, a full complement of legal assistants, and superior support personnel, Levene, Gouldin & Thompson has the resources and the depth to assure clients of complete representation and necessary expertise in matters ranging from the conventional to the highly complex.

The stately brick office building which is the home of Levene, Gouldin & Thompson, LLP gives an aura of strength and stability. Photo by Carriage House Photography.

The lawyers of Levene, Gouldin & Thompson enjoy an enviable state-wide reputation, both among other lawyers and with the judiciary. *Martindale-Hubbell,* the national peer review reference journal, accords the firm its highest rating, and a number of attorneys are listed in *Best Lawyers in America.* Many of the firm's attorneys have been asked to lead various State Bar Association specialty sections and serve as instructors at programs designed to provide continuing education for the profession.

The firm has handled matters in almost every county in the state, as well as many jurisdictions beyond the borders of New York. Although the firm has represented numerous Fortune 500 companies in some of their legal mattters and is sensitive to the fact that we are functioning in an increasingly global marketplace, the real strength of the firm derives from its work with the area's local businesses and individual clients. The strong, positive image of Levene, Gouldin & Thompson emanates from its commitment to competence and its concern for the community.

Dating back to the beginning of this century, when many immigrant families came to the area to establish their homes, Broome County residents became known for their work ethic and their pride in their

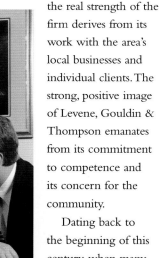

Offering prompt, practical, result-oriented counsel has made Levene, Gouldin & Thompson one of the largest and most respected law offices in the state of New York. Photo by Carriage House Photography.

products. Those values became a part of the ethic for most businesses in the community. Levene, Gouldin & Thompson, which dates its origins to 1927, owes much of its reputation for integrity and hard work to the traditions already established in this community when David Levene first established the practice.

The firm's concern for the community is reflected in the commitment of its lawyers and staff to civic activities in the area. The firm's recognition that we all owe more to this exceptional community than we can ever repay has been part of the motivation for individuals assuming leadership roles in major cultural, educational, and charitable organizations, and also supporting civic activities at the grassroots level as door-to-door fund-raisers, den mothers, walkathon participants, troop leaders, coaches, and chaperones, to name just a few.

While respectful and committed to the valued traditions of the past, Levene, Gouldin & Thompson has a progressive outlook reflected not only by its commitment to continuing education, but also by its efforts to obtain maximum benefit from the latest in available technology. The synergy of the teamwork concept at Levene, Gouldin & Thompson is enhanced by the sophisticated, state-of-the-art network that affords immediate interaction with all members of the staff and permits clients to have the benefit of available expertise beyond the scope possessed by the individual with whom they may be working most directly.

Whether advising a local business owner about business development and tax planning, counseling a senior citizen about the legal consequences of aging, helping an individual or family buy a new home, or representing an accident victim seeking just compensation for personal injuries, the lawyers at Levene, Gouldin & Thompson are committed to pursuing a standard of excellence while "giving back" to the community in which their families are fortunate to live and prosper. ■

Norman J. Davies, Architect

There are times when life just works out right—as it has for Norman J. Davies, Architect. He is the owner of a firm that is exactly where it wants to be—a small group capable of large accomplishments. Since its establishment in 1968, the company has been providing quality architectural, engineering, and interior

One of the strengths of the Norman J. Davies firm is flexibility in providing solutions and giving guidance in all phases of architecture, design, and planning. The Cullman Day Care Center is a fine example of the firm's work.

design services for the Built Environment. Davies believes that if his firm does a good job, a reasonable income will follow. He has always been more interested in providing functional, aesthetically pleasing, cost-effective, energy-efficient, handicapped-accessible buildings than in how much the project generates in dollars.

With a staff of seven professionals, five of whom are full-time employees, the group is large enough to handle substantial ventures and yet small enough to provide personal attention for projects of a smaller scale. Many years of experience has made them aware of the need to be creative, technically competent, and keenly responsive to client needs.

The company philosophy is to offer the same intensive service to everyone who requests help, whether it is a small renovation or a major work. Because Norman Davies and his staff make the building experience easy and enjoyable, they have many clients of long standing. One of their most gratifying creations has been the Kennedy-Willis Center on Down Syndrome at Pathfinder

Village in Edmeston, New York. Every room was developed with a positive aura of brightness and peace, to soothe the mind and lighten the spirit.

Another customer who repeatedly trusts the talent and expertise of the Davies organization is The At-A-Glance Group in Sidney, New York, whose buildings reflect strength and modern technology. They are also architects for the prestigious National Soccer Hall of Fame in Oneonta, New York.

A key element in all buildings completed by the Davies firm is attention to handicapped accessibility; special measures are taken to devise appropriate mainstream access for everyone.

Some of Davies' favorite designs are for places of worship. He has studied and traveled extensively throughout the world with the Interfaith Forum on Religion, Art, and Architecture. Every religious edifice designed by the Davies firm projects an ambiance of elements that together present a sacred venue for spiritual growth. By allowing a freedom of space, augmented with color, texture, and lighting, the buildings inspire an uplifting reverence.

One of the strengths of the Norman J. Davies firm is flexibility in providing solutions and giving guidance in all phases of architecture, design, and planning. Clients have confidence in the team, who can properly articulate a project and meet architectural needs with distinction. Corporate membership in the American Institute of Architects offers employees opportunities for continuing education and guidelines for maintaining excellence in technical aptitudes and service.

The excitement of producing structures built with insight and care will continue for the Norman J. Davies firm as it looks forward to meeting the challenges of each day, dealing with interesting people, and keeping the "art in architecture." ∎

The Norman J. Davies firm was the architect for the prestigious National Soccer Hall of Fame in Oneonta, New York.

c h a p t e r

BUILDING GREATER
BROOME COUNTY

New York State Electric & Gas Corporation (NYSEG)

New York State Electric & Gas Corporation (NYSEG) has come a long way. Today, it sells electricity and natural gas to 1 million customers across more than 40% of upstate New York. NYSEG's revenues are $2.5 billion a year, based on annual sales of 36 million megawatt-hours of electricity and 62 million dekatherms of natural gas.

THE BEGINNING

NYSEG's current status stands in strong contrast to its modest beginnings in 1852, when a few businessmen pooled $75,000 to sell gas lighting in Ithaca. Since Ithaca was then an important coal shipping center, the new Ithaca Gas Light Company used coal to make its gas. The coal was baked in a series of brick ovens, and the gas it gave off was stored in a large holder that had to be filled by dusk each day to light the gas lamps. Just as the railroads had their "gandy dancers," so gas manufacturing had its "gas house gang" who shoveled coal in 12-hour shifts seven days a week. It was a smelly, grimy job that only the toughest could handle.

Thirty years later lighting was revolutionized by the electric bulb, and gas use declined until the turn of the century when new uses were found for it in industry and for heating and cooking in the home. Today, natural gas has replaced manufactured gas, and NYSEG distributes natural gas but no longer produces it. Electric

Electricity spread rapidly in the 1880s and 1890s as shown by downtown Binghamton in 1895.

street lighting spread during the 1880s and 1890s to Binghamton, Ithaca, Elmira, Auburn, and beyond, and with Thomas Edison's invention of the incandescent light bulb, electricity entered the home—at first as single drop lights that operated only at night.

During the 1890s neighboring electric companies began merging with the Ithaca gas company, and in 1916 it changed its name to the Ithaca Gas & Electric Corporation. As the demand for electricity accelerated, further consolidations took place, and in 1929 the company became the New York State Electric & Gas Corporation. By 1937 its electric service area had reached its present size. In 1949 NYSEG became investor-owned when General Public Utilities Corporation sold all 880,000 shares of NYSEG stock to the public.

THE ENERGY DELIVERY PROVIDER

NYSEG works hard to provide superior customer service and reliability. "NYSEG, the energy people you can count on" is more than just a slogan; for the company it's a way of life. NYSEG has established a Call Center in Binghamton to handle customers' phone calls quickly and effectively. NYSEG has achieved the lowest customer complaint rate in New York State, and it constantly receives high marks for customer service, as shown by its almost 100-percent success in meeting its service guarantees. To keep its customers informed, NYSEG has set up an exciting Web site that includes on-line meter reading, weather forecasts, and construction updates that tell travelers where they may experience delays or parking restrictions.

BUSINESS EVOLUTION

For many years NYSEG produced most of its own electricity—mainly at coal-fired generating stations that were rated among the most efficient in the nation. Two of its major power plants, Kintigh near Niagara Falls and Milliken north of Ithaca, were nationally recognized for their efficiency and environmental leadership. Both plants demonstrated NYSEG's commitment to a clean environment by using scrubbers to remove sulfur dioxide they would otherwise emit and by adjusting boilers to reduce nitrogen oxide emissions.

In other measures to protect the environment, NYSEG has cleaned up gas manufacturing sites its predecessor companies used many, many years ago, removed polychlorinated biphenyl (PCB) capacitors, and reduced PCB concentrations in substation transformers and regulators. It has also been a leader in converting vehicles to natural gas and finding valuable uses for the fly ash and bottom ash produced by its power plants.

COMMUNITY COMMITMENT

Serving the community remains a high priority with NYSEG, and its employees play a large role in improving the quality of life in areas the company serves. NYSEG provides financial support, and its employees perform thousands of hours of volunteer work for worthwhile organizations ranging from fire departments to youth organizations. Employees clean up roads under the state's Adopt-A-Highway program, support colleges, and help students through NYSEG's education services. Under the Community Watch program, employees report emergencies, accidents, fires, and suspicious or unsafe activities to police or fire departments.

NYSEG assists low-income customers through Project SHARE, which provides grants to help them pay heating bills or make emergency repairs to heating equipment. The company's innovative Power Partner program helps customers pay off their arrears and conserve energy.

COMPETITION

Today, NYSEG is changing as its industry changes. Competition has already spread through the natural gas industry and is now transforming the nation's electric utilities. While NYSEG will continue to be the sole distributor of electricity to homes and businesses in its service area, the production and supply of power are being opened up to other companies. NYSEG has sold its coal-fired power plants and is giving its customers the opportunity to switch to other electricity suppliers. NYSEG is now the primary subsidiary of a holding company, Energy East Corporation, which is developing energy-related businesses across the Northeast. NYSEG's strategy for the new competitive era is superior customer service, operational excellence, and business growth.

With residential natural gas prices frozen since late 1995, NYSEG's natural gas is highly competitive throughout the Northeast, and the company has become a leader in adding new natural gas franchises because of its reputation for superior customer service. NYSEG's success in getting customers to convert to natural gas from other fuels is 10 times that of other natural gas companies, again because of its reputation for service.

Throughout its long history, NYSEG has striven to improve the efficiency and quality of people's lives and businesses while also meeting the utility industry's highest standards of operating excellence, customer service, and integrity. ■

NYSEG restored power fast after a tornado struck Binghamton at the end of May 1998.

Newman Development Group

The Newman family is reinventing retail sites in Broome County and acquiring a reputation as solid as the structures they create. Since 1986, the father-son team of Barry and Marc Newman has been leading the The Newman Development Group. David Newman has recently joined the family force, bringing expertise as an attorney and management specialist. Encompassing both a real estate company and a construction corporation, they are dedicated to recapturing economic outflow, and creating jobs. The dynamic development organization specializes in transformations from eyesore to economic asset.

Facilities, such as Town Square Mall in Vestal, New York, created by the Newmans are more than just places to shop—they are community centers enriching lives with opportunity. Photo by Carriage House Photography.

Their ever expanding portfolio is bringing new life and vitality into stagnant industrial sites and derelict shopping centers by revitalizing, remodeling, releasing, and situating national retail tenants in appropriate settings. Numerous undertakings in and around Broome County have been pursued and successfully completed.

In 1992 NDG's "flagship venture," The Town Square Mall in Vestal, New York, was opened. Encompassing over 600,000 square feet of new retail space, the mall has become a crown jewel in the local employment market. This center will be undergoing dramatic changes in 1999, increasing excitement about "progress on the Parkway." Expansion plans have recently been approved allowing Wal-Mart to grow from a standard store format to a Supercenter. Additionally, Barnes & Noble will relocate from their current position to a new freestanding and much larger facility.

Translating ideas into reality has not come easily. Several years of patience, diplomacy, and meticulous work in planning and gaining approvals went into a process that has yielded ongoing benefits for the people of the area by increasing access to major retailers and giving a giant boost to the economy. NDG's vision for the future is to continue being a dominant force as quality developers for national retailers.

Extensive lease negotiations handled by Marc Newman and a gigantic construction program orchestrated by Barry Newman set the stage for the first Lowe's Home Improvement Warehouse in New York State. In 1996 the impressive facility opened adjacent to the Town Square Mall.

The Binghamton market is benefiting from another creative concept from the Newmans. The Front Street "Gardens," with close access to Interstate 81, is being developed for a 12-screen stadium movie theater, a Cracker Barrel Restaurant, and a Marriott Fairfield Inn complex.

Newman acquisitions are being enhanced by even more property on the Vestal Parkway, and amazing changes will be part of redevelopment slated to begin in December 2000. Currently, their reach spreads through four mid-Atlantic states and will be expanding to eight states over the next three to five years.

The business is a team effort, comprised of a dedicated staff encompassing engineering, CAD operations, demographic analysis, and environmental and property management professionals. A full complement of related support personnel give NDG the background to complete all projects on schedule and within budget, while gaining respect for courtesy and competence.

Facilities created by the Newmans are more than just places to shop—they are community centers enriching lives with opportunity. ∎

Encompassing both a real estate company and a construction corporation, Newman Development Group is dedicated to recapturing economic outflow, and creating jobs. One such project is Parkway Plaza in Vestal, New York.

Robert A. Mead & Associates, Inc.

Robert A. Mead & Associates, Inc. is the premier resource for commercial real estate services in the Southern Tier of New York and northern Pennsylvania. Exclusively serving the needs of the business community, it has become the acknowledged leader in all phases of commercial/industrial real estate.

President and founder of the corporation, Robert A. Mead has over 20 years of real estate experience, including a diverse background in real estate development. In 1996 he obtained the SIOR designation, awarded only to those in the industry who reach the highest level of achievement and professionalism. In spite of dramatic changes in the commercial real estate arena, influenced by technology and economic conditions, the combined strengths of Mead and his staff have dominated the fields of commercial real estate sales/leasing, appraisals, consulting, and project development.

Adding to the distinctive array of assistance offered to clients, is BridgeMark Services, Inc., formed by Mead in 1993. It is a specialized marketing and disposition consulting firm to provide information to its Fortune 100 clients, including IBM, Lockheed Martin, SONY, and Stanley Works.

Robert A. Mead & Associates is also the exclusive representative for New America International (NAI) in the Southern Tier. NAI incorporates more than 150 member firms and 210 offices worldwide, giving access to a greater national and international presence. This membership facilitates close cooperation among affiliate brokerages across the country. As active participants in the network's concept of corporate services, seamless coverage is made possible for corporate clients whose needs for acquisition or disposition span a wide geographic area and multiple sites. International consultation and service is conveniently available, while performed locally.

A totally innovative concept devised by the agency is a custom-designed commercial/industrial computerized database. It is the only one of its kind in the area. This is the heart of its commercial/industrial brokerage operation. By aggressively combining experienced personnel, marketing resources, and an exclusive information network, accurate information and investment analysis are instantaneously obtainable. Clients reap the benefits of dealing with professionals who respond quickly with answers geared to their specific requirements. Robert A. Mead & Associates is the only source in the region for a database of comparables in the commercial market. For anyone who needs to know about Broome County's commercial real estate, the statistics in this database are essential.

Sophisticated techniques and teamwork were used in a "build-to-suit" development group formed by Mead in 1992. Development projects successfully completed during recent years include hotels, luxury townhouses, industrial parks, fast-food restaurants, office buildings, and distribution facilities. No other real estate organization has done more to revitalize the local economy, by bringing employment back to the "Valley of Opportunity."

With an excellent balance of progressive networking and up-to-the-minute technology, Robert A. Mead & Associates is held in high esteem across the nation. It is noteworthy that a company of this size is able to compete with major organizations on an international scale to provide marketing solutions. Creativity and diligence foster a business environment that encourages prompt, friendly customer-centered commercial real estate services. Robert A. Mead & Associates facilitates the responsible transfer of ownership and development of an area's most lasting resource—real estate—thereby strengthening the economic structure and future of the community. ∎

Robert A. Mead & Associates, Inc. is the premier resource for commercial real estate services in the Southern Tier of New York and northern Pennsylvania. Photo by Carriage House Photography.

Evans Mechanical, Inc.

For five generations the name "Evans" has been synonymous with quality plumbing and heating services. The roots of this company can be found in the classic American dream. In 1917 Silas Evans started the company in Scranton, Pennsylvania. In 1923 he brought his wife and daughter to Broome County determined to build his own plumbing enterprise. Toting his tools around town in a wheelbarrow, Silas soon became a familiar figure on the streets of Endicott. His diligence, pride in quality workmanship, and excellent service are the legacy of today's Evans Mechanical. Specializing in industrial and commercial contracting, the company is still owned and run by the Evans family. Silas's grandson Karl and Karl's daughter and son-in-law, Susan and J.B. Barnes, are current owners. Two of J.B. and Susan's children, Josh and Jessyca, are the fifth generation to be active in the company.

Prefabrication capabilities is an example of the cutting-edge technology used on intricate piping systems.

The business has come a long way from a one-man shop to becoming an official, privately held corporation in 1960. There are now 50 to 60 employees, depending on seasonal fluctuations, all kept busy serving Broome County and areas within an hour's radius of their home office at 314 Maple Street, Endicott, New York.

The firm is experienced in mechanical contracting for industrial, commercial, and institutional buildings, municipal utility facilities, and power plants. A broad range of mechanical services, including piping, plumbing and heating, sheet metal, sprinkler, and temperature control are a few of the complete circle of services offered.

Adapting to the growing needs of specialized functions, Evans is certified by the highest standards providing certified welders, certified medical gas installers and installation, and back flow prevention system testing and repairs. But this is only part of the impressive array of unique expertise available. The company can also handle any kind of fire protection work, environmental site remediation, and underground tank replacement.

Every project undertaken by Evans Mechanical is entered with the goal of continuing quality assistance beyond the initial completion. Their dedication to long-term relationships with customers has earned them a well-deserved presence in many major industries, local school districts, and hospitals. The Broome County Fuel Management System and the Broome County Landfill have both benefited from Evans' technologically superior performance.

The firm often participates with the owner and general contractor during the planning of projects by providing value engineering and budget services. On competitively bid plan and specification work, the company is a knowledgeable prime contractor and subcontractor of process piping, HVAC, and plumbing operations.

Prefabrication capabilities on their home site is an example of the cutting-edge technology used on intricate piping systems. The finished product often resembles a huge geometric work of art, which, in fact, it is—created by masters of industrial arts. Piping systems are the conveyers of community success and comfort.

Evans Mechanical is union oriented and a signatory contractor with Local 112, Plumbers and Steamfitters. Evans also maintains membership in many professional associations that promote high standards and ethics. With excellent financial backing, a bond capacity that allows corporate growth, and a reputation for fair and competent treatment of all parties associated with their construction projects, Evans is in a position to furnish all solutions as a mechanical contractor. ∎

Certified welding is performed for every need.

Air Temp Heating & Air-Conditioning, Inc.

Air Temp Heating & Air-Conditioning, Inc. is a mechancial HVAC service/construction and energy management company. Family owned and nationally affiliated, the organization has always taken pride in providing a full complement of mechanical system applications from its Broome County headquarters.

Air Temp Heating & Air-Conditioning, Inc. is a mechancial HVAC service/construction and energy management company. Photo by Carriage House Photography.

Located at 1165 Front Street in Binghamton, the company has a significant impact on local development, as well as areas throughout New York State and northern Pennsylvania. Through a service franchise with The LINC Corporation, its affiliation extends to the top 150 mechanical service contractors in the world. This connection makes national resources available to assist Air Temp to efficiently manage and control all customer HVAC requirements. Tailored maintenance agreements ranging from scheduled inspection services to "on-site" operating arrangements are a specialty. Through use of LINC'S exclusive Assured Business Efficiency software, Air Temp is able to specify and schedule maintenance tasks by drawing from an exhaustive manufacturer's database that covers every kind of HVAC equipment.

Mechanical systems are complex, requiring specialized skills to install and to maintain efficiency. Air Temp provides single source responsibility and professional service 24 hours a day, seven days a week. Customers have the security of expert technicians who can respond to any emergency, any time. Air Temp is able to offer customized programs to design, build, and install HVAC systems to meet any specialized requirement. Everything from standard environmental control systems to clean rooms requiring constant temperature and humidity control is available for today's state-of-the-art buildings. These total environment systems create energy savings and optimize comfort levels to increase productivity in the workplace.

Air Temp is knowledgeable in every phase of duct fabrication and installation, and has the capacity to design and construct ductwork and other specialty sheet metal accessories in its own technologically advanced facility. As part of its full-service approach, system air balancing is also offered. As an authorized Novar controls dealer, Air Temp has available the most cost-effective methods to keep mechanical systems operating efficiently, with prudent energy use and reducing operating costs.

An example of Air Temp's dedicated commitment to being a caring corporate partner was the donation of labor and materials for the heating and air-conditioning systems at the Police sub-station built on Liberty Street in Binghamton. And, as members of the American Society of Heating, Refrigerating and Air Conditioning Engineers, Inc. (ASHRAE), Air Temp continues to contribute to the public good by supporting the advancement of the arts and sciences in HVAC&R technology. Membership in several professional trade associations offers educational opportunities and recognition of excellence for the firm and its employees—working together—and finding better ways to serve customers with dynamic management practices.

Using a fleet of over 30 service vehicles and a staff of highly trained individuals, Air Temp considers every day an opportunity to exercise high standards, integrity, honesty, and effectiveness in serving its customers. Air Temp has an old-world pride in workmanship that is an established part of its business profile. ∎

Using a fleet of over 30 service vehicles and a staff of highly trained individuals, Air Temp considers every day an opportunity to exercise high standards, integrity, honesty, and effectiveness in serving its customers. Photo by Carriage House Photography.

Kradjian Enterprises

For over 70 years the Kradjian name has been associated with opportunity and entrepreneurial spirit. In 1917, two teenage brothers emigrated from Armenia to Binghamton, New York. With hard work and the American Dream, the two brothers saved the money they earned and invested in a small dry cleaning company. With a "can-do" attitude, the Kradjians grew the dry cleaning business, bought out competitors, and eventually purchased Bates Troy Laundry, which has been in operation since 1852.

Housed in a Laurel Avenue facility in Binghamton, Bates Troy Quality Dry Cleaning & Laundry is now the largest two-phased operation of its kind in the Southern Tier. The Bates Troy Health Care Linen Services, the fastest growing division of this industry, specializes in the linen needs of health care facilities and institutions within a 100-mile radius. Bates Troy Laundry has recently acquired the state-of-the-art European LAVATECH Tunnel washing system. Through this equipment, the quality of service and cost containment that Bates Troy provides is unparalleled in today's stringent health care environment.

For over 70 years the Kradjian name has been associated with opportunity and entrepreneurial spirit.

From this prospering business, the Kradjians and their children began their second business: developing real estate throughout the country. Kradjian Properties is the property development company which is helping revitalize Broome County real estate. Kradjian Properties specializes in office, retail, and residential development. Among its notable achievements are Downtown Binghamton Development, The West Side of Binghamton Revitalization of Main Street, and the current Highlands Development in Vestal. Other accomplishments include the Vestal Executive Office Park, University Square Plaza, the historical Press Building, Plaza 5, Holiday Inn Suny, the Galleria Center, and Metrocenter in Binghamton.

Three generations of Kradjians are involved in the management of this community-based enterprise today. The Kradjians all have been supportive of community projects and often participate in leadership positions. The most recent contribution includes helping launch the much acclaimed First Night Binghamton Annual New Year's Eve community celebration. The Kradjians are still building upon their family heritage to revitalize and improve the quality of life in this beloved area. ■

c h a p t e r

14

HEALTH CARE & EDUCATION

Lourdes Hospital

In 1925, the Corbett mansion on Riverside Drive (the site of the current Lourdes main campus) became home to a 25-bed hospital. Bishop Daniel Curley of the Syracuse Diocese asked the Daughters of Charity, pioneers in Catholic health and hospital service, to come to Binghamton to manage the new hospital, which was purchased with funds contributed by concerned citizens.

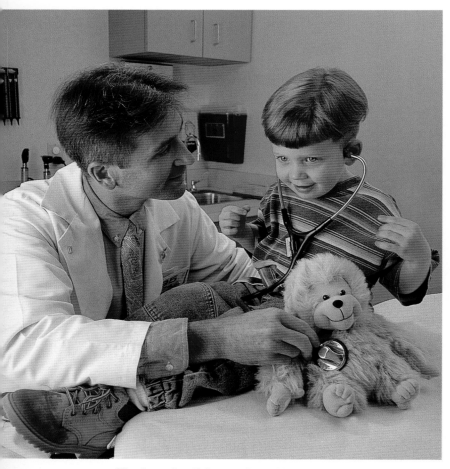

The Lourdes Primary Care Network consists of over 20 physician offices and walk-in services throughout the Southern Tier.

Today, the Daughters of Charity National Health System is one of the largest nonprofit health care providers in the nation with 60 health care facilities, including 46 acute-care hospitals that it owns or cosponsors in 15 states and the District of Columbia.

With the commitment of the Daughters through Lourdes, the Southern Tier got its first recovery room, first intensive care unit, first Hospice, first Pain Management Center, first Electrodiagnostic Laboratory, and the Regional Cancer Center, whose reputation earned it an affiliation with the prestigious Johns Hopkins Oncology Center. These are just some of the many contributions Lourdes has made as a cornerstone community institution. In recent years, Lourdes has looked beyond the hospital campus, establishing primary care sites throughout the region and making

health care portable and accessible with its Mission in Motion vehicles.

For over 40 years, Lourdes Regional Cancer Center has been recognized as a leader in cancer care, offering a comprehensive program of services from education and cancer prevention through state-of-the-art detection, diagnosis, treatment, and continuing care. The center is staffed by an interdisciplinary team of board-certified oncology doctors, nationally certified oncology nurses, and medical physicists and therapists. The Cancer Center has also been recognized by the American College of Surgeons, Commission on Cancer, for efforts in cancer care and ranks among the largest and most sophisticated community cancer centers in the country.

Continuing its commitment to prevention and early diagnosis, Lourdes Regional Cancer Center developed a comprehensive Cancer Prevention and Detection Program. The program is designed to assist men and women of all ages with concerns about cancer and cancer risk. The cancer screening program includes physical exams designed to detect cancer early, advice on ways to prevent cancer, information on tests and exams geared toward early detection, instruction on self-exam prevention techniques, and free cancer information.

The Cancer Center is also a major sponsor of the American Cancer Society's Relay for Life, a popular community event which raises funds and promotes cancer survivorship. Lourdes Breast Care Center promotes breast cancer awareness by sponsoring special programs every October during Breast Cancer Awareness Month.

In an effort to move beyond the traditional medical model of health care and improve the overall health of the community it

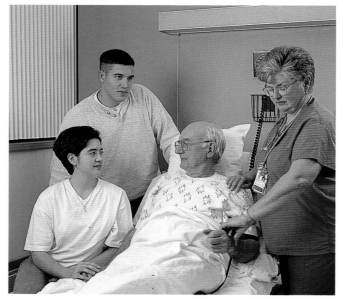

Putting patients' needs first is accomplished at Lourdes through patient-focused care and case management.

Lourdes has looked beyond the hospital campus, establishing primary care sites throughout the region and making health care portable and accessible with its Mission in Motion vehicles.

serves, Lourdes purchased two mobile medical vans. The mobile vans, dubbed "Mission in Motion," are equipped to provide breast exams, mammograms, screenings, primary care, immunizations, dental care, and many other services. Those who live in remote areas, or who have transportation problems, and the poor are often unable to reach many hospital-based services. The mobile units bring needed health care services to those who are medically underserved.

Further improving access to medical care is Lourdes Primary Care Network, consisting of over 20 physician offices and walk-in services throughout the Southern Tier. The physicians and allied health professionals of the network are dedicated to providing high quality, accessible, patient-centered care.

Offering the latest technology in outpatient surgery in a comfortable, convenient setting is the Lourdes Ambulatory Surgery Center. The Center, which opened in December 1997, includes an ophthalmology and laser center, a new GI lab, three minor procedure rooms, and private patient rooms adjacent to Lourdes' main operating rooms. The Ambulatory Surgery Center is designed with the patient and physician needs in mind, providing convenient access to the highest quality outpatient surgical services available.

Rounding out Lourdes' list of comprehensive health care services is Lourdes Wellness Center, which offers over 90 innovative health enhancement courses as well as complementary health services. The Arthritis Center uses a team approach to the management of arthritis, lupus, fibromyalgia, osteoporosis, and other musculoskeletal conditions. Lourdes Center for Outpatient Diabetes Education is the only diabetes program in the region certified by the American Diabetes Association. Meanwhile, affiliation with the prestigious Diabetes Treatment Center of America has positioned Lourdes as the region's premier diabetes treatment program. The Behavioral Health program offers a wide range of services to assist with mental health and alcohol or substance abuse problems.

The Wound Care Center uses advanced techniques and therapies to develop treatment programs designed to fit each patient's individual needs. Maximizing patients' abilities and quality of life is the mission of Lourdes Rehabilitation Services, which offers occupational, physical, and speech therapy. A Center for

Orthopedic Care specializes in the care of knees, hips, shoulders, feet, and spine. Lourdes' commitment to the community's future is realized through a comprehensive Youth Services program designed to help children and youth develop healthy behaviors, and to strengthen families.

Putting patients' needs first is accomplished at Lourdes through patient-focused care and case management. At Lourdes the patient is the center of all activities, rather than a passive recipient of services. Quality service and effective resource utilization are seen as part of patients' rights.

Much has changed in the community and at Lourdes since a small 25-bed hospital opened on Riverside Drive more than 70 years ago, but there remains one constant: the commitment of the Daughters of Charity and their mission of caring. Combining this mission with the latest technology has helped Lourdes earn the reputation as a "high-touch" and "high-tech" health care provider. Explore the many excellent health care services Lourdes provides. ■

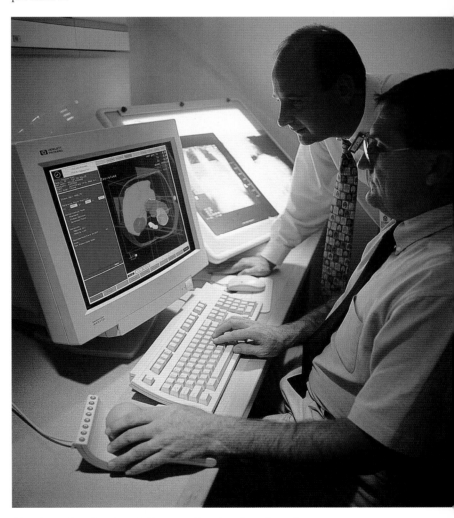

The Lourdes Regional Cancer Center developed a comprehensive Cancer Prevention and Detection Program designed to assist men and women of all ages with concerns about cancer and cancer risk.

Binghamton University,
State University of New York

Acclaimed as one of the preeminent public universities in the nation, Binghamton University offers an Ivy-caliber education at one of the country's best educational values. Nationally recognized for its strong academic programs, distinguished faculty, and talented students, Binghamton University combines the best attributes of a growing research institution with the intimacy of a small liberal arts college.

Located amid the rolling hills of the Susquehanna River Valley, the beautiful, modern campus blends rural and urban life with an excellent research library, outstanding computer facilities, a superb performing arts center, a multiclimate teaching greenhouse, and a 117-acre Nature Preserve.

The institution dates from 1946, when the Triple Cities College opened in Endicott, New York, as a branch of Syracuse University to meet the educational needs of local veterans returning from World War II. Four years later it was incorporated into the State University of New York system and renamed Harpur College. In 1961, the campus moved across the river to its current location in Vestal, and in 1965, Binghamton became one of four

Binghamton enrolls more than 12,000 students in programs leading to bachelors's, master's, and doctoral degrees in the liberal arts and sciences, management, nursing, education and human development, and engineering and applied science.

doctoral-granting University Centers in the SUNY system and was formally renamed the State University of New York at Binghamton.

The University annually enrolls in excess of 12,000 students in more than 130 programs leading to bachelor's, master's, and doctoral degrees. The University's curriculum, founded in the liberal arts, has expanded to include selected professional and graduate programs. Fifteen specialized research centers attract scholars from around the globe.

Harpur College of Arts and Sciences offers fields of study and research in the humanities, social sciences, and science and mathematics. Four professional schools round out the academic offerings. The School of Education and Human Development provides study for careers in teacher education, human development, counseling, and public service. The School of Management educates students in finance, accounting, and management. The Decker School of Nursing provides an unsurpassed nursing curriculum with concentrations in family nursing, community health, and gerontological care. The Watson School of Engineering and Applied Science offers graduate and undergraduate study in computer science, electrical engineering, mechanical engineering, and systems science and industrial engineering.

The five colleges work together to create an intellectually exciting university that has been noted for distinguished scholars, rigorous and challenging courses, and highly rated graduate and professional programs.

With nearly 20,000 students seeking admission each year, Binghamton leads all other SUNY institutions in applications. Admitted students are among the best and brightest in New York State and beyond. More than half graduate in the top 10 percent of their high school class, and their SAT scores are typically 250 points above the national average.

Students benefit from the careful oversight of a dedicated, experienced faculty, of whom more than 30 hold the rank of

Binghamton University's modern campus is situated on a wooded hillside overlooking the Susquehanna River. Acclaimed as one of the best public universities in the nation, Binghamton is recognized for its strong academic programs, distinguished faculty, and talented students.

As one of the four research and doctoral universities of the State University of New York, Binghamton has grown into a highly regarded research university, but it has retained the collegial qualities of a smaller school.

Distinguished Professor. Professors actively engage students in teaching and research at the undergraduate and graduate levels. The faculty work closely with students in the residence halls as part of Binghamton's living/learning programs and serve as mentors to freshmen in a program that draws critical praise from observers in higher education.

All undergraduates receive a grounding in the liberal arts that encourages communication skills, global awareness, and first-hand research. Innovative programs explore and strengthen links between disciplines. One such program is the Science Across the Curriculum project, which exposes students in scholarly fields as diverse as English and music to scientific principles.

The University also places an emphasis on international education. More than 1,900 international students come to study on campus from 89 nations, while Binghamton students study at universities on five continents. On campus, programs encourage students to pursue language and cultural studies and international experiences, regardless of their major.

The University is committed to using technology to support its academic initiatives. Internet connections are available in every residence hall room, "smart classrooms" allow faculty to enhance lectures with state-of-the-art visuals, and technology lets students travel the globe to investigate distant places or pursue distance learning.

Beyond the classroom, students can take advantage of numerous recreational and cultural activities. Student athletes compete and excel in 19 sports as part of the NCAA's Division II and are frequent Academic All-Americans. Weight rooms, swimming pools, racquetball and tennis courts, indoor and outdoor tracks, and two gymnasia serve students and the community. Six distinct libraries house more than 3.6 million items.

Binghamton's commitment to excellence can be measured in part by the success of its more than 65,000 graduates who have become leaders in the arts and sciences, in human services, and in business. They are physicians and teachers, nurses and engineers, artists and actors. Each year, more than 400 firms come to campus to recruit new graduates.

Beyond its educational enterprise, Binghamton participates in the life of the Southern Tier in many ways. It is a valued economic resource, contributing more than $300 million to the local economy each year, and is the second largest employer in the area during the academic year.

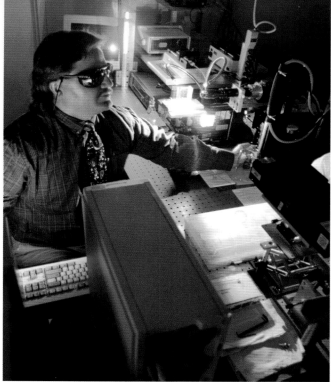

Fifteen specialized research centers attract scholars from around the globe. University scholars collaborate with industrial and community partners on a number of projects.

Its cultural and sporting activities enrich community life. The world-class Anderson Center for the Arts showcases major U.S. and foreign symphony orchestras and dance ensembles. The music and theater departments offer more than 100 concerts and productions yearly. The University Art Museum, with a permanent collection of 1,500 objects, is supplemented by traveling and loaned exhibits.

Students and faculty contribute hundreds of hours in numerous research and service projects with local schools, health care, and social service agencies. The University's Small Business Development Center and the Trade Adjustment Assistance Center are vital partners with regional industry. The Watson School works with companies across the state through its Integrated Electronic Engineering Center and the Strategic Partnership for Industrial Resurgence. The Public Archaeology Facility conducts archaeological surveys for major public works projects. The Psychology Department's Institute for Child Development serves children who require intensive emotional, behavioral, social, and communication intervention.

Binghamton's commitment to effectiveness, innovation, and excellence has been rewarded with generous contributions from alumni, friends, and supporters. The University's endowment, which has more than doubled in the last few years, is now one of the largest in the SUNY system.

A rapidly changing higher education environment demands a cooperative and adaptive spirit, as well as the foresight to take risks and embark on bold new initiatives. This premise is being ably met. Touted as the crown jewel of the State University of New York system, Binghamton University is fulfilling the dreams of its founders, continuing to grow and excel. ■

United Health Services

A century of quality health care in Broome County has gone into the formation of United Health Services. It is a family of health service organizations existing to serve the community by developing and maintaining a comprehensive and cost-effective regional health system.

United Health Services was formed in 1981 as a not-for-profit organization by the consolidation of several hospitals in the area—beginning a new era of medical excellence.

In 1887 a group of citizens met to discuss the hospital requirements for the people of Binghamton. It took until 1888 for a house to finally be selected as suitable for the purpose. The building was located on what was described as a "most commanding and beautiful site, healthful and pleasant for all the unfortunate victims of accident and disease," and stitches were sewn into the fabric of history, creating Binghamton General Hospital.

The year 1905 saw The Kings Daughters of Lestershire enlisting the assistance of the great local industrialist and philanthropist George F. Johnson in making medical care available in this neighboring town. Johnson donated a house to serve as a hospital. In 1916 the village name changed to Johnson City, and in 1926 the hospital became the Charles S. Wilson Memorial Hospital, a general, nonprofit entity. From these roots the United Health Services of today has been created.

United Health Services is currently a more than 700-bed teaching hospital and health care system, made up of United Health Services Hospitals, Chenango Memorial Hospital, Delaware Valley Hospital, Ideal Senior Living Center, Good Shepherd-Fairview Home, and United Home Health. It is affiliated with United Medical Associates, P.C., a group medical practice, and with the United Health Services Foundation. Consolidation of the facilities and functions has been a joining of assets, producing savings and enhancing health care service capacity. New alignments are continuously being considered and evaluated for local and regional partnerships.

United Health Services is a recognized medical leader in the community—the largest provider and second largest employer in the county. Always striving for excellence led to the first open heart surgery program in Broome County, developed through an affiliation with the Presbyterian Hospital in the City of New York. United Health Services is also the only trauma center for the region and has an on-site helipad for medevac missions.

United Health Services Hospitals is a major teaching affiliate of the Clinical Campus at Binghamton of the State University of New York's Health Science Center at Syracuse. As such, it plays an important role in educating tomorrow's medical professionals and ensuring that the community's supply of physicians and allied health associates keeps pace with technological advances. A commitment to teaching is evident in the United Health Services Center for Community Health, where a philosophy of assisting individuals to achieve happier, healthier, and more productive lives is put into action with education and prevention information. "Stay Healthy" courses are offered, as well as free access to the area's largest health library, physician referrals, insurance counseling, and services for people with special health needs. United Health Services also operates a large web site, www.uhs.net.

In order to expand services and develop programs in response to the needs of the population, such as in mental health, renal dialysis, chemical dependency, and physical rehabilitation, United Health Services is progressive in holding down costs, and

In 1887 citizens met to discuss the hospital requirements for the people of Binghamton. It took until 1888 for a house to finally be selected as suitable for the purpose for Binghamton General Hospital.

throughout its history has been willing to sacrifice to make this possible. To provide high-quality care that is also affordable, United Health Services has formed innovative partnerships with more than 200 of the community's top physicians and with health insurance plans to give patients the greatest value in services.

Millions of dollars are being invested to modernize and maintain technological superiority at all facilities. These innovative approaches have led the way to introducing new, less invasive surgical procedures, helping to minimize pain and speed recovery. State-of-the-art diagnostic equipment detects diseases sooner than ever before. And United Health Services has been the regional innovator in strategic coordination of the medical industry, seamlessly coordinating teams of health specialists to work with patients and families who require extraordinary medical or

United Health Services is affiliated with United Medical Associates, P.C., a group medical practice.

United Health Services was formed in 1981 as a not-for-profit organization by the consolidation of several hospitals in the area—beginning a new era of medical excellence.

surgical care. This is part of the corporate belief in tailoring services and programs for each person and situation.

Striving always to blend technological advances in medicine with a warm, human touch for patients and their families is part of a philosophy of caring. Wisdom and knowledge are used in extending dignity, sensitivity, and respect to every individual. The success of this health network is a mix of teamwork, cooperation, and collegiality set in an environment of mutual trust and open dialogue.

The United Health Services health care organization is owned by the community, and exists solely to make the healing arts available to everyone. It is directed, and its policies are set, by local boards whose members serve without monetary compensation. To ensure that no one is denied care, United Health Services is committed to serving the poor and those without the means to pay. This significant mission is essential to the overall well-being of society.

United Health Services is the basis for the strong medical infrastructure available in the Twin Tiers region. Existing as the nerve center and heart of the area's health care systems, the United Health Services mission is achieved by people of the community serving their friends and neighbors.

United Health Services is dedicated to meeting an ever-changing array of health care needs, from the beginning of life through the golden years, in the new century and beyond. ∎

Binghamton Psychiatric Center

The year was 1858, and the New York State Inebriate Asylum was established as the first in the nation. On a peaceful hilltop of 252 acres overlooking the Susquehanna River Valley, a tradition of innovation in medical care began. To house the revolutionary facility, architect Isaac Perry created a magnificent castellated Gothic edifice. He built with dramatic gray stone, a castle complete with towers, turrets, and buttresses, a structure that still dominates the complex. In 1879 a broadening of perspective led to changes, and the asylum was rededicated as a facility for the insane. And in 1997 the castle was designated a National Historic Landmark. Today, the Binghamton Psychiatric Center continues the tradition of innovation in caring for people with mental health needs.

For more than a century, progressive psychiatric care through BPC has been available to people in an ever-widening catchment area in the south central part of New York. Treatment has changed over the years, leading to the current underlying principle that we are all partners in the recovery of patients with serious and persistent mental illness—patients, family, and community, working together to provide respectful quality treatment at the least restrictive level of care.

There are many facets that make BPC unique, including an impressive array of services for individuals at any stage of life. From adolescence through the geriatric years, professional teams of skilled medical and rehabilitation personnel provide treatment, rehabilitation, guidance, and support to individuals with serious and persistent mental illness, and offer programs and services geared to meet their specific needs.

Emphasis is placed on providing services which enable the individual to remain in the community.

Progressive psychiatric care through BPC is available to people in an ever-widening catchment area in the south central part of New York.

The Adolescent Crisis Residence (ACR) serves youths 13 through 17 who are in situational crisis or who are working in treatment in the community and are in need of a brief scheduled respite. The ACR's main goal is to help youths avert hospitalization and assist youths in remaining out of long-term residential placements.

The Adolescent Day Treatment Program treats and educates severely emotionally and psychiatrically disturbed adolescents, which enables them to remain in the community. It provides the highest level of outpatient care and a comprehensive array of services.

The Children and Youth Mobile Mental Health Team provides consultation and assessment services for children from birth through 17 years of age for non-mental health agencies. The team also makes mental health treatment service linkages as needed and provides mental health in-services for the staff of the agencies they serve. This valuable service promotes early detection of developing mental health needs in children, thus providing critical early intervention which helps maintain them with their families in the community.

The Adult Situational Crisis Residence (ASCR) provides crisis intervention, health, medication education, short-term counseling, and stress management services to adults 18 years of age or older who are experiencing crisis in their home or environment. These short-term services focus on averting the crisis and maintaining the individual in the community.

For those individuals requiring more intense inpatient psychiatric care, the Adult Admission Service is available. Individuals receive services which facilitate stabilization of symptoms for timely discharge, as well as being taught the skills necessary to live in a community setting.

The Adolescent Day Treatment Program augments assistance for youth and offers the highest level of outpatient care for youngsters.

Through the Hilltop Industries Program, local industries supply work for which patient participants are paid while they are building the skills required to leave the program for community employment.

A Community Preparation Unit is available for seriously and persistently mentally ill persons ages 18 and older . This Unit functions as a predischarge program which facilitates movement of persistently ill inpatients to a successful community living situation of their choice. The quality of life for patients is improved with supervision and training in all areas of daily living.

A Family Care Residential Program allows individuals 18 or older to maximize his or her potential while residing in the community. Care takes place in a private home, where advice and assistance in daily living skills are provided. Case management support is provided by specially trained staff.

The Family Support and Advocacy Program's main goal is to educate family members about mental illness and to provide an open forum for discussion and exchange of ideas. This strengthens the partnership between family and staff in devising appropriate measures to facilitate recovery.

The specialized needs of older citizens are the focus of the Geriatric Treatment Service, which provides inpatient psychiatric care for the elderly aged 65 and older. The Geriatric Mobile Team provides screening and evaluation services to potential patients to make a determination of need for admission to inpatient services.

Both adult and geriatric patients residing in the community who are recovering from mental illness can receive treatment services at the Continuing Treatment and Rehabilitation Center through either the BPC Outpatient Clinic or services available through the PrePaid Mental Health Plan(PMHP). PMHP is a managed care program for behavioral health which promotes individual recovery with an emphasis on creating hope within the treatment and rehabilitation process. Promoting success in community living is a primary focus of the services available to PMHP enrollees. A multidisciplinary staff consisting of professionals in the fields of psychiatry, nursing, psychology, social work, and rehabilitation work closely with each individual to design a

plan for treatment and rehabilitation tailored to their needs.

Complementing this level of care is the CHOICES program, the only NYS licensed and certified Intensive Psychiatric Rehabilitation Treatment Program in Broome County. CHOICES, IPRT is a unique rehabilitation service provided for individuals with major mental illness seeking more satisfying and successful life roles. The emphasis is to assist individuals who want to make changes in their roles within the living, learning, working, or social environments to be able to choose, get, and keep the changes they aspire to make.

Vocational Rehabilitation Services at BPC provides a wide array of opportunities and services to patients from all populations served by the facility. Dedicated professional rehabilitation staff provide assessment and evaluation, support and counseling, job readiness activities, and paid work. Individuals are encouraged to develop work skills through participation in paid work. They are also involved in individual and group activities which help them identify their vocational goals.

The Hilltop Industries Program represents a unique collaboration between BPC and local industry. Local industries supply work for which patient participants are paid while they are building the skills required to leave the program for community employment.

Perhaps the most original vocational program is the Cobbler's Bench Store. Originally established in 1973, it is now located in the Metrocenter in downtown Binghamton. Quality products and services are manufactured and sold by program participants. The consumer-run retail business is thriving, featuring fine wood furniture, Balloon Bouquets, and related accessories.

The Assisted Competitive Employment Program offers job development and job coaching services to those individuals ready to make the transition to community-based employment. Work has a tremendous impact upon the recovery process and results in a greater level of independence. Additionally, paid work provides the opportunity for friendships, challenges, and an increase in self-confidence.

The mind is a wondrous, delicate balance of the physical, emotional, and spiritual. Binghamton Psychiatric Center has for decades recognized these human intricacies and the curative power of collaborative efforts dedicated to restoring individuals with serious and persistent mental illness to their desired roles in the community. ■

The Cobbler's Bench Store is a consumer-operated business in downtown Binghamton.

United Methodist Homes

The United Methodist Homes of the Wyoming Conference has managed programs and services for the elderly since 1958. Currently, the Homes operates five facility sites, serving nearly 1,500 residents and employing over 1,000 individuals.

The Homes' facilities provide a wide variety of services designed to meet the social, spiritual, and physical needs of each resident while encouraging as much independence as possible.

The Homes operates under a "continuum of care" concept which features various levels of living that allow for movement through the system if it becomes necessary. In the event of deteriorating health, comprehensive treatment can be provided (based upon availability), preventing the need to uproot from familiar surroundings. These services, however, cannot totally replace those provided in the acute care hospital setting.

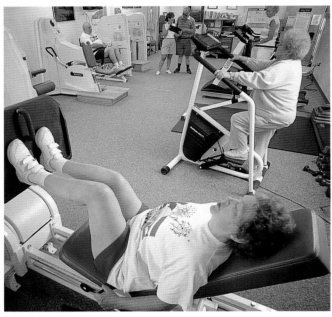

Residents enjoy a complete wellness center, utilizing strength and conditioning programs designed specifically for seniors.

In the Broome County area the Homes operates two facilities: Elizabeth Church Manor Retirement Community and Hilltop Retirement Community. At these locations, the Homes provides lifestyle options ranging from two-bedroom townhouses to complete nursing care.

Residents may also avail themselves of complete wellness centers, utilizing strength and conditioning programs designed specifically for seniors. Social activities are organized by a trained and caring staff. Special events and outings are planned throughout the year. Opportunities are always available for those who choose to participate. Certified social workers are on site to offer support and address concerns of residents and family members. Resident Council gives all those living in the Homes the opportunity to voice opinions on a regular basis. An active chaplaincy program is available to attend to the spiritual needs of the residents.

The Homes is a not-for-profit corporation that is governed by an elected board of directors that represents a broad base of individuals from the various communities which it serves.

Admission to the Homes is open to all seniors, regardless of religious affiliation, race, color, age, sex, handicap, or source of payment. ■

The United Methodist Homes' facilities provide a wide variety of services designed to meet the social, spiritual, and physical needs of each resident while encouraging as much independence as possible.

Broome Community College

Since 1946, Broome Community College (BCC) has been serving the region's educational, training, and lifelong learning needs with the philosophy of quality service to the community. With 40 associate degree programs, designed either for transfer or career preparation, an ever-expanding offering of workforce development certificates, corporate service training designed for company employees, and hundreds of vocational and avocational community courses, the college truly pulses with opportunities for various audiences on its modern, well-equipped campus.

The degree programs are divided into five categories, offering a comprehensive selection of university parallel Associate in Arts or Science degrees and career preparation Associate in Applied Science degrees; engineering, technology, and computing; allied health science programs; liberal arts; business; and public service programs.

Since 1946, Broome Community College (BCC) has been serving the region's educational, training, and lifelong learning needs with the philosophy of quality service to the community.

Introductory versions of many of these degree programs are available as certificates. Additional certificates, such as Medical Transcription and Dental Assisting, are designed as a complement to the region's current workforce development needs.

BCC's faculty is a mix of full-time, experienced professors and part-time teachers. In most programs, faculty are assisted by advisory councils of community members giving curriculum guidance.

Study, on campus, in one of the college's 15 buildings, is the traditional approach for participants to reach their goals. However, an increasing number of courses are now available on-line for students to use the computer anywhere, anytime, to access courses.

Each year the college enrolls over 5,000 full- and part-time students, most from the Broome County area, in its credit programs. The average age is 23 for full-time students and 31 for

Each year the college enrolls over 5,000 full- and part-time students, most from the Broome County area, in its credit programs. The average age is 23 for full-time students and 31 for part-time students.

part-time students. About half of BCC graduates transfer to four-year schools. To facilitate this, BCC has established articulation agreements with dozens of private and public colleges ensuring full credit transfer.

Additionally, BCC participates in the guaranteed transfer program with SUNY four-year schools. The other half of the graduates put their new skills immediately to use by joining the area workforce.

BCC has also been an asset to economic development via its Community Education and Corporate Service offices. Dozens of local companies yearly contract with the college for on-campus, or on-company site management and employee training needs. Nearly 2,000 employees a year participate in this program. Additionally, the publicly advertised non-credit community education program of hundreds of job-related or personal improvement courses is attended by over 8,000 people.

Since moving to its present location on Upper Front Street in 1957, BCC has continually built new facilities and remodeled its original structures. The recent modernization includes the Applied Technology Building, the rebuilt Paul F. Titchener Hall, and, most recently, the ultramodern Dr. G. Clifford and Florence B. Decker Health Science Center with its high quality hospital/clinic facilities. Currently, BCC is building a major expansion of its Student Center to include all new activities spaces and an indoor ice rink. This new building will be the heart of BCC's student life, which already includes 13 varsity sports and over 50 clubs ranging from Student Government and professional affiliates to honor societies and social organizations.

As it moves into the twenty-first century, BCC will do even more to reaffirm service to its community of students and businesses. This dynamic institution will continue to redefine itself, to celebrate its successes, and to embrace its new challenges. ■

BIBLIOGRAPHY

Domin, Gail. "The Carousels of Broome County." *Yorker Magazine*, Volume 4, Winter, 1996, Number 2.

Hammond, Karen. *From Vision to Excellence: A Popular History of Binghamton University*. Virginia Beach, VA: The Donning Company/Publishers, 1996.

Seward, William Foote, ed. *Binghamton and Broome County, New York: A History*. 3 vols. New York: Lewis Historical Publishing Company, 1924.

Smith, Gerald R. *The Valley of Opportunity: A Pictorial History of the Greater Binghamton Area*. Virginia Beach, VA: The Donning Company/Publishers, 1988.

Smith, H.P., ed. *History of Broome County, N.Y.* Vol. 1. Syracuse, New York: D. Mason and Company, 1885.

Versaggi, Nina M. *Hunter to Farmer: 10,000 Years of Susquehanna Prehistory*. Binghamton, New York: Roberson Center for the Arts and Sciences, 1986.

OTHER RESOURCES

"A History of Ross Park." Broome County Historical Society, 1985.

"Binghamton Centennial Booklet, 1867-1987."

"1897 Illustrated Binghamton." Annual souvenir booklet issued by The Binghamton Railroad Company.

"Milestones 1776-1976." A publication of the *Sun-Bulletin*, 1976.

The Press & Sun-Bulletin. Various issues

Inside (Binghamton University campus newspaper). Various issues

Broome Chamber web site at www.spectra.net/broomechamber

ACKNOWLEDGEMENTS

Readers who find *Broome County Images* intriguing will want to visit one or more of the area's fine libraries, virtually all of which contain fascinating books and pamphlets about the area from its earliest days to the present, profiles and biographies of notable Broome County residents, and corporate and institutional profiles.

In writing *Broome County Images*, I drew on the expertise of several people who generously advised me on specific chapters. I especially appreciate the assistance of Broome County Historian Gerald R. Smith who gave freely of his time to help me polish the history chapter, and Gail Domin of Susquehanna Heritage Area at the Binghamton Visitor's Center for reading the carousel chapter and sharing her knowledge about these Broome County landmarks.

I am grateful to Nina M. Versaggi, Director of the Public Archaeology Facility at Binghamton University, for providing fascinating information about the county's prehistory, to Village of Johnson City Historian Janet Ottman for background information and anecdotes about the carousels, and to Kim Eaton of Tri-Cities Opera and Stephen Raube-Wilson of the Binghamton Philharmonic for providing me with a wealth of information. Special thanks to lifelong Broome County resident Bob Bromley of Vestal for sharing his wide-ranging knowledge of Broome County sports and leisure activities.

I am indebted to the Broome County Chamber, including Chairman of the Board David Birchenough, President and CEO Richard J. Lutovsky, and Communications Manager Karen Troidl for sponsoring this book and for being among its most enthusiastic supporters.

A sincere thank you to my good friend and freelancing colleague Sue Rosenberg for her unfailing eye and always trenchant advice.

And finally, thanks to my family—my husband, Nat, for his forbearance as yet another project overflowed my home office and spilled into his life, my daughter Emily for her Generation X insights into Broome County, and my son Gregory, whose astute observations and suggestions were always on target and contributed greatly to the timely completion of the manuscript.

I hope that current residents of Broome County, those who contemplate establishing homes or businesses here, and former residents who continue to hold the beautiful valley in their hearts will enjoy these images of Broome County today.

Karen Hammond

ENTERPRISE INDEX

IBM Endicott
1701 North Street
Endicott, NY 13760
Phone: 607-755-0123
Pages 140-141

Kradjian Enterprises
84 Court Street, Suite 600
Binghamton, NY 13901
Phone: 607-722-1135
Fax: 607-722-0147
Page 182

Levene, Gouldin & Thompson, LLP
450 Plaza Drive
Vestal, NY 13850
Mailing Address:
Post Office Box F-1706
Binghamton, NY 13902-0106
Phone: 607-763-9200
Fax: 607-763-9211
www.lgt@llp.com
Page 172

Lockheed Martin Control Systems
600 Main Street
Johnson City, NY 13790
Phone: 607-770-2000
Fax: 607-770-5771
E-Mail: webmaster@lmcontrolsystems.com
www.lmcontrolsystems.com
Pages 144-145

Lockheed Martin Federal Systems, Owego
1801 State Route 17C
Owego, NY 13827
Phone: 607-751-2000
www.owego.com
Pages 142-143

Lourdes Hospital
169 Riverside Drive
Binghamton, NY 13905
Phone: 607-798-5111
Fax: 607-798-7681
www.lourdes.com
Pages 186-187

McFarland-Johnson, Inc.
171 Front Street
Binghamton, NY 13905
Phone: 607-723-9421
Fax: 607-723-4979
E-Mail: mcfarland@mjinc.com
www.mjinc.com
Page 168

National Pipe & Plastics, Inc.
3421 Old Vestal Road
Vestal, NY 13850
Phone: 607-729-9381
Fax: 607-729-6130
www.nationalpipe.com
Pages 132-133

New York State Electric & Gas Corporation (NYSEG)
Corporate Drive
Kirkwood Industrial Park
Post Office Box 5224
Binghamton, NY 13902-5224
Phone: 800-572-1131
www.nyseg.com
Pages 176-177

Newman Development Group
3101 Shippers Road
Vestal, NY 13851
Phone: 607-770-1010
Fax: 607-777-9464
E-Mail: newmandev@aol.com
www.newmandevelopment.com
Page 178

Norman J. Davies, Architect
783 Chenango Street
Binghamton, NY 13901
Phone: 607-724-8882
Fax: 607-772-4142
Page 173

The Raymond Corporation
Post Office Box 130
Greene, NY 13778
Phone: 607-656-2311
Fax: 607-656-9005
E-Mail: marcom@raymondcorp.com
www.raymondcorp.com
Page 134

Raytheon
Post Office Box 1237
Binghamton, NY 13902-1237
Phone: 607-721-5465
Fax: 607-721-4742
E-Mail: kmanderson@hti.com
www.raytheon.com
Pages 148-149

Robert A. Mead & Associates, Inc.
111 Grant Avenue, Suite 103
Endicott, NY 13760
Phone : 607-754-5990
Fax: 607-754-7826
E-Mail: raminc@sieba.com
Page 179

Security Mutual Life Insurance Company of New York
Post Office Box 1625
100 Court Street
Binghamton, NY 13902
Phone: 607-723-3551
Fax: 607-724-1607
www.smlny.com
Pages 158-159

Tri-Town Insurance
Corporate Offices
192 Front Street
Owego, NY 13827
Phone: 607-785-1300
Fax: 607-687-5338
www.tritowninsurance.com
Page 163

United Health Services
10-42 Mitchell Avenue
Binghamton, NY 13903
Phone: 607-762-2336
Fax: 607-762-2631
www.uhs.net
Pages 190-191

United Methodist Homes
700 Harry L. Drive
Post Office Box 316
Johnson City, NY 13790
Phone: 607-798-1001
Fax: 607-798-0095
E-Mail: kte@pronetisp.net
www.norwich.net/umhwc
Page 194

Universal Instruments Corporation
Post Office Box 825
Binghamton, NY 13905
Phone: 607-779-7740
Fax: 607-779-4510
Pages 146-147

Visions Federal Credit Union
24 McKinley Avenue
Endicott, NY 13760
Phone: 607-754-7900
Fax: 607-754-9772
www.visionsfcu.org
Page 162

PATRONS

Binghamton Simulator Company, Inc.
Broome-Tioga BOCES
Columbian Mutual Life Insurance Company
CTSI
Don's Automotive Mall, Inc.
Loomis Tax Service
Piaker & Lyons, P.C.

Photo by Van Zandbergen Photography.

INDEX

Photos by Van Zandbergen Photography.

Photos by Van Zandbergen Photography.

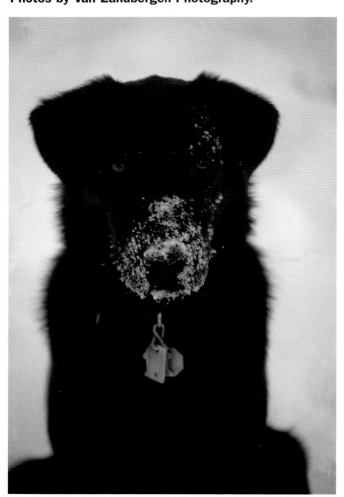

Photos by Van Zandbergen Photography.